Gluten-Free Crock Pot Cookbook for Beginners

2000 Days of Easy, Healthy, and Irresistible Slow Cooker Creations – Your Ultimate Guide to Crafting Delicious Gluten-Free Recipes!

Tharne Dllsworth

Table of Contents

INTRODUCTION

Benefits of a Crock Pot

The crock pot, also known as a slow cooker, has become an indispensable kitchen appliance for many households due to its numerous benefits. Here are some key advantages of using a crock pot:

Time Efficiency:

One of the primary benefits of a crock pot is its time-saving convenience. This appliance allows individuals to prepare meals with minimal hands-on time. Once the ingredients are placed in the pot and the timer is set, the slow cooking process begins, allowing individuals to focus on other tasks or activities. This is particularly advantageous for individuals with busy schedules, as they can return home to a fully cooked, delicious meal without the need for constant monitoring.

Tender and Flavorful Dishes:

The slow cooking process of a crock pot is ideal for breaking down tough cuts of meat and creating tender, flavorful dishes. The low and slow cooking method allows proteins to slowly absorb the flavors of herbs, spices, and other ingredients, resulting in rich, complex flavors. This makes the crock pot a perfect tool for preparing stews, braises, and soups.

Energy Efficiency:

Crock pots are energy-efficient appliances. Compared to traditional ovens and stovetops that may consume more electricity, a crock pot uses less energy over an extended period. The long, slow cooking process at lower temperatures contributes to energy conservation, making it an eco-friendly option for cooking.

Versatility in Ingredients:

Another advantage of the crock pot is its versatility in accommodating a wide range of ingredients. From vegetables and meats to legumes and grains, the slow cooker allows for the preparation of diverse recipes. This versatility is especially valuable for those following specific dietary restrictions, such as a gluten-free diet, as it provides the flexibility to create flavorful and satisfying meals without compromising dietary needs.

Hands-Free Cooking:

Unlike traditional cooking methods that may require constant attention, a crock pot allows for hands-free cooking. Once the ingredients are assembled, individuals can simply set the timer and let the slow cooker do the work. This hands-free approach is beneficial for individuals who may not have the time or inclination to stand over a stove or oven.

Economical Meal Preparation:

Crock pots are excellent tools for economical meal preparation. They make it easy to utilize less expensive cuts of meat, as the slow cooking process helps tenderize and enhance the flavors of more budget-friendly options. Additionally, the ability to cook in larger quantities allows for leftovers, reducing the need for frequent cooking and saving both time and money.

Convenience for Batch Cooking:

The crock pot's large capacity makes it ideal for batch cooking. Individuals can prepare sizable quantities of food and freeze portions for later consumption. This is particularly advantageous for those who prefer to plan and prepare meals in advance, ensuring a constant supply of homemade, ready-to-eat dishes.

In conclusion, the crock pot is a versatile and time-saving appliance that offers numerous benefits for individuals seeking a convenient and efficient way to prepare delicious meals. Its ability to enhance flavors, accommodate various ingredients, and promote hands-free cooking makes it a valuable asset in any kitchen. Whether for busy professionals, families, or individuals with dietary restrictions like gluten-free diets, the crock pot stands out as a reliable and practical cooking solution.

Gluten Intolerance vs. Gluten Allergy

In the realm of dietary considerations, gluten intolerance and gluten allergy represent two distinct yet often misunderstood conditions. Both conditions involve adverse reactions to gluten, a protein found in wheat, barley, and rye, but they manifest differently in terms of symptoms, severity, and long-term health implications.

Gluten Intolerance: Unraveling the Complexities

Gluten intolerance, commonly known as non-celiac gluten sensitivity (NCGS), is a condition characterized by gastrointestinal and/or extra-intestinal symptoms triggered by the consumption of gluten. Unlike celiac disease, gluten intolerance does not involve the immune system attacking the small intestine. Individuals with gluten intolerance may experience symptoms such as bloating, abdominal pain, diarrhea, fatigue, and headaches. However, these symptoms are generally less severe than those associated with celiac disease.

One of the challenges in identifying gluten intolerance lies in the absence of standardized diagnostic markers. Unlike celiac disease, which can be confirmed through specific blood tests and intestinal biopsies, gluten intolerance is often diagnosed by the exclusion of other conditions and the observation of symptom improvement on a gluten-free diet. This lack of definitive diagnostic tools has led to skepticism in some medical circles, making it essential for individuals suspecting gluten intolerance to work closely with healthcare professionals.

From a culinary perspective, managing gluten intolerance involves a focus on gluten-free alternatives. In the realm of crock pot cooking, this translates to selecting gluten-free grains, such as rice, quinoa, and corn, and using gluten-free thickeners like cornstarch or arrowroot. Crock pot recipes can easily be adapted by replacing traditional wheat-based ingredients with gluten-free alternatives, allowing individuals with gluten intolerance to enjoy a diverse and flavorful array of dishes.

Gluten Allergy: A Immunological Battle

On the other hand, gluten allergy, commonly referred to as wheat allergy, is an immune-mediated response to specific proteins in wheat. Unlike gluten intolerance, which is primarily a digestive issue, gluten allergy involves the immune system producing antibodies (IgE) in response to wheat proteins. Symptoms of a gluten allergy can range from mild, such as hives and itching, to severe, including anaphylaxis, a life-threatening allergic reaction.

For individuals with a gluten allergy, the avoidance of wheat and wheat-derived products is non-negotiable. From a culinary standpoint, this means meticulous scrutiny of ingredient labels to identify hidden sources of wheat, such as modified food starch, hydrolyzed vegetable protein, and certain sauces and condiments. In the context of crock pot cooking, special attention must be paid to broths, seasonings, and thickening agents, as they may contain wheat derivatives. Utilizing gluten-free substitutes and being vigilant about cross-contamination are imperative to ensure the safety of individuals with a gluten allergy.

In conclusion, understanding the distinction between gluten intolerance and gluten allergy is crucial for both individuals affected by these conditions and the culinary professionals catering to their dietary needs. While gluten intolerance involves a range of symptoms, often centered around the digestive system, gluten allergy is an immune response that can have life-threatening consequences. From a culinary perspective, accommodating both conditions in a gluten-free crock pot cookbook requires careful ingredient selection, substitution, and a keen awareness of potential sources of gluten. By embracing the nuances of gluten-related disorders, we can create inclusive and delicious culinary experiences for everyone, regardless of their gluten sensitivity.

The Science behind a Gluten Free Diet

The popularity of gluten-free diets has grown significantly in recent years, with many people adopting this dietary approach for various reasons, including celiac disease, gluten sensitivity, and a desire for a perceived healthier lifestyle. Understanding the science behind a gluten-free diet is crucial for those who choose or need to follow it.

Gluten is a complex mixture of proteins found in wheat, barley, rye, and their derivatives. The two main proteins in gluten are gliadin and glutenin, and it is the gliadin component that triggers an immune response in individuals with celiac disease. Celiac disease is an autoimmune disorder in which the ingestion of gluten leads to damage in the small intestine, impairing nutrient absorption. This can result in a range of symptoms, from digestive issues to fatigue and skin problems.

For individuals with celiac disease, following a strict gluten-free diet is the only effective treatment. Even small amounts of gluten can trigger an immune response and cause damage to the small intestine. Gluten sensitivity, a condition where individuals experience symptoms similar to those of celiac disease without the autoimmune response, also requires a gluten-free diet for symptom relief.

Beyond these medical conditions, some people choose a gluten-free diet as a lifestyle choice. However, it's essential to note that a gluten-free diet, if not done carefully, can lack certain nutrients present in gluten-containing grains. Whole grains like wheat, barley, and rye provide essential vitamins, minerals, and fiber. Therefore, individuals on a gluten-free diet should pay careful attention to ensuring they obtain these nutrients from alternative sources.

Gluten-free flours, such as those made from rice, corn, quinoa, and almond, can be used as substitutes for traditional wheat flour in cooking and baking. It's important to read labels carefully, as many processed foods may contain hidden sources of gluten. Cross-contamination is also a concern, particularly in shared

kitchen spaces or when dining out. Therefore, individuals with celiac disease must be diligent in avoiding not only direct sources of gluten but also potential cross-contamination.

While a gluten-free diet is essential for those with celiac disease or gluten sensitivity, it's important to recognize that it may not necessarily be a healthier choice for everyone. Gluten-free processed foods can sometimes be higher in sugar and fat to compensate for the lack of gluten, potentially leading to an unbalanced diet. As with any dietary change, consulting with a healthcare professional or nutritionist is advisable to ensure that nutritional needs are met.

In conclusion, the science behind a gluten-free diet revolves around understanding the role of gluten in triggering immune responses in certain individuals. For those with celiac disease or gluten sensitivity, strict adherence to a gluten-free diet is vital for managing symptoms and preventing long-term health complications. However, individuals considering a gluten-free lifestyle should do so with awareness, ensuring they maintain a balanced and nutritious diet.

Tips and Tricks to Make Gluten-Free Crock Pot Dishes Easier

Adopting a gluten-free diet doesn't mean sacrificing the convenience and flavors associated with hearty, slow-cooked meals. With the right tips and tricks, making gluten-free crock pot dishes can be both easy and delicious.

- Choose Gluten-Free Ingredients:

  Begin by selecting gluten-free ingredients for your crock pot recipes. Ensure that the spices, broths, sauces, and other flavorings you use are free from gluten-containing additives. Read labels carefully, as gluten can sometimes hide in unexpected places.

- Use Naturally Gluten-Free Grains:

  Explore alternative grains that are naturally gluten-free, such as quinoa, rice, millet, and buckwheat. These grains can be excellent substitutes for gluten-containing grains in your crock pot dishes, providing a nutritious and satisfying base.

- Experiment with Gluten-Free Flours:

  When thickening sauces or soups, traditional wheat flour is often used. However, there are plenty of gluten-free flour options available, such as rice flour, chickpea flour, or cornstarch. Experiment with these alternatives to achieve the desired consistency in your crock pot recipes.

- Be Mindful of Cross-Contamination:

  Prevent cross-contamination by thoroughly cleaning all utensils, cutting boards, and surfaces before preparing gluten-free crock pot meals. If possible, designate specific kitchen tools for gluten-free cooking to reduce the risk of accidental contamination.

- Utilize Naturally Gluten-Free Proteins:

  Focus on protein sources that are naturally gluten-free, such as poultry, fish, beef, pork, legumes, and tofu. These options can be easily incorporated into various crock pot recipes, providing a hearty and satisfying meal.

- Readily Available Gluten-Free Broths and Stocks:

  Many store-bought broths and stocks may contain gluten, so it's essential to choose gluten-free options. Alternatively, you can make your own broth at home using gluten-free ingredients like vegetables, herbs, and gluten-free meat.

- Explore Gluten-Free Condiments and Sauces:

  Common condiments and sauces may contain gluten, but there are gluten-

free alternatives readily available. Check labels for gluten-free soy sauce, Worcestershire sauce, and other flavor enhancers to add depth to your crock pot dishes.

- Opt for Whole, Unprocessed Foods:

  Focus on whole, unprocessed foods in your gluten-free crock pot cooking. Fresh vegetables, lean meats, and gluten-free grains are not only healthier but also reduce the risk of unintentional gluten exposure.

- Invest in Gluten-Free Spice Blends:

  Spice blends can be a quick way to add flavor to your dishes, but some may contain gluten. Look for certified gluten-free spice blends or create your own using individual gluten-free herbs and spices.

- Convert Favorite Recipes to Gluten-Free Versions:

  Don't be afraid to adapt your favorite crock pot recipes to make them gluten-free. Experiment with alternative ingredients and adjust cooking times to suit gluten-free substitutions.

By incorporating these tips and tricks, you can enjoy the convenience and richness of gluten-free crock pot dishes without compromising flavor or texture.

With a bit of creativity and a commitment to using gluten-free ingredients, your slow-cooked meals can become a highlight of your gluten-free culinary experience.

Take Care of Your Crock Pot

Caring for your Crock Pot is essential to ensure its longevity and optimal performance. Proper maintenance not only enhances the efficiency of the appliance but also guarantees the safety of your food preparation. Here's a comprehensive guide on how to take care of your Crock Pot:

- Cleaning:

    One of the most crucial aspects of Crock Pot care is regular cleaning. After each use, allow the appliance to cool down before cleaning. Most Crock Pots have removable stoneware inserts and lids that can be washed in the dishwasher. However, always refer to the manufacturer's instructions for specific cleaning guidelines. If your Crock Pot is not dishwasher safe, wash the components with warm, soapy water, and use a non-abrasive sponge to avoid scratching the surfaces.

- Handling and Storage:

    When handling the stoneware insert, be cautious to prevent any accidental damage. Avoid drastic temperature changes, such as placing hot stoneware

Removeable Stoneware

Stainless Steel Finish

Dishwasher Safe Stoneware & Lid

Low, High, and Warm Settings

on a cold surface, as this may cause cracks. When storing your Crock Pot, ensure it is clean and completely dry. Store the stoneware and lid separately to prevent any unwanted odors from lingering.

- Exterior Maintenance:

  Wipe down the exterior of the Crock Pot with a damp cloth after each use to remove any spills or splatters. Avoid using abrasive cleaners or scouring pads, as they may damage the finish. Pay attention to the control panel, and gently clean it with a damp cloth if necessary. Be cautious not to let any liquid seep into the control panel or electrical components.

- Lid Care:

  The lid is a critical component for retaining heat and flavors in your recipes. Clean the lid thoroughly after each use, as food residue can accumulate and affect the taste of future dishes. Some Crock Pot lids are dishwasher safe, but always check the manufacturer's instructions. If handwashing, use a soft sponge to prevent scratching. Additionally, ensure the vent holes are clear to allow steam to escape during cooking.

- Avoid Abrasive Utensils:

  When stirring or serving food from your Crock Pot, use non-metallic utensils to prevent scratching the stoneware insert. Metal utensils can damage the non-stick coating on some inserts and lead to premature wear.

- Temperature Checks:

  Periodically check the temperature

settings of your Crock Pot to ensure accuracy. You can do this by using an external food thermometer to verify that the temperature inside the pot matches the selected setting. If you notice any discrepancies, it may be a sign that your Crock Pot needs professional attention.

- Storage Tips:

  If you plan to store your Crock Pot for an extended period, make sure it is completely dry and clean. Store it in a cool, dry place, and cover it to prevent dust accumulation. Before using it again, inspect the power cord for any signs of damage and check that all components are in good condition.

- Regular Inspections:

  Conduct regular visual inspections of your Crock Pot for any signs of wear, damage, or malfunction. Look for frayed cords, cracks in the stoneware, or any issues with the control panel. If you notice anything unusual, contact the manufacturer or a qualified technician for advice.

By following these guidelines, you can ensure that your Crock Pot remains in top-notch condition, providing you with delicious and hassle-free meals for years to come. Regular care and maintenance not only extend the life of your appliance but also contribute to the overall safety and quality of your cooking experience.

Chapter 1: Breakfast & Brunch

Blueberry Almond Oatmeal

Prep Time: 10 Minutes   Cook Time: 3 Hours   Serves: 4

Ingredients:

- 2 cups gluten-free rolled oats
- 4 cups almond milk
- 1 cup fresh or frozen blueberries
- 1/2 cup sliced almonds
- 1/4 cup maple syrup
- 1 teaspoon vanilla extract
- Pinch of salt

Directions:

1. In the slow cooker, combine rolled oats, almond milk, blueberries, sliced almonds, maple syrup, vanilla extract, and a pinch of salt.
2. Stir well, cover, and cook on low for 3 hours or until the oats are tender.
3. Stir before serving and top with additional blueberries and almonds if desired.

Nutritional Value (Amount per Serving):

Calories: 310; Fat: 6.64; Carb: 71.72; Protein: 9.85

Slow Cooker Banana Nut Bread Pudding

Prep Time: 20 Minutes   Cook Time: 3 Hours   Serves: 8

Ingredients:

- 1 loaf gluten-free banana bread, cubed
- 3 ripe bananas, mashed
- 4 large eggs, beaten
- 2 cups almond milk
- 1/2 cup chopped walnuts
- 1/4 cup maple syrup
- 1 teaspoon cinnamon
- 1/2 teaspoon vanilla extract
- Pinch of salt

Directions:

1. Grease the slow cooker with cooking spray.
2. In a large bowl, combine banana bread cubes, mashed bananas, beaten eggs, almond milk, chopped walnuts, maple syrup, cinnamon, vanilla extract, and a pinch of salt.
3. Mix well and transfer to the slow cooker.
4. Cover and cook on low for 3 hours or until the pudding is set.
5. Serve warm, optionally topped with a dollop of dairy-free whipped cream.

Nutritional Value (Amount per Serving):

Calories: 181; Fat: 8.51; Carb: 25.07; Protein: 3.05

Slow Cooker Apple Cinnamon Quinoa Porridge

Prep Time: 15 Minutes   Cook Time: 3 Hours   Serves: 6

Ingredients:

- 1 cup quinoa, rinsed
- 3 cups unsweetened almond milk
- 2 apples, peeled and diced
- 1/2 cup raisins
- 1 teaspoon ground cinnamon
- 1/4 cup chopped pecans
- 2 tablespoons maple syrup
- Pinch of salt

Directions:

1. Rinse the quinoa under cold water and drain.
2. In the slow cooker, combine quinoa, almond milk, diced apples, raisins, cinnamon, chopped pecans, maple syrup, and a pinch of salt.
3. Stir well, cover, and cook on low for 3 hours or until the quinoa is tender.
4. Stir before serving and adjust sweetness if needed.

Nutritional Value (Amount per Serving):

Calories: 243; Fat: 6.31; Carb: 43.24; Protein: 5.31

Overnight Slow Cooker Pumpkin Spice Oatmeal

Prep Time: 10 Minutes   Cook Time: 8 Hours   Serves: 6

Ingredients:

- 2 cups gluten-free rolled oats
- 4 cups almond milk
- 1 cup canned pumpkin puree
- 1/4 cup maple syrup
- 1 teaspoon pumpkin spice
- 1/2 teaspoon vanilla extract
- Pinch of salt
- Pecans or pepitas for topping

Directions:

1. In the slow cooker, combine rolled oats, almond milk, pumpkin puree, maple syrup, pumpkin spice, vanilla extract, and a pinch of salt.
2. Stir well, cover, and cook on low for 8 hours.
3. Stir before serving and top with pecans or pepitas.

Nutritional Value (Amount per Serving):

Calories: 230; Fat: 6.76; Carb: 48.57; Protein: 7.21

Slow Cooker Cranberry Orange Quinoa Porridge

Prep Time: 15 Minutes   Cook Time: 3 Hours   Serves: 6

Ingredients:

- 1 cup quinoa, rinsed
- 3 cups orange juice
- 1 cup fresh cranberries
- 1/2 cup chopped pecans
- 1/4 cup honey or maple syrup
- 1 teaspoon vanilla extract
- Pinch of salt
- Orange zest for garnish

Directions:

1. Rinse the quinoa under cold water and drain.
2. In the slow cooker, combine quinoa, orange juice, fresh cranberries, chopped pecans, honey or maple syrup, vanilla extract, and a pinch of salt.
3. Stir well, cover, and cook on low for 3 hours or until the quinoa is tender.
4. Stir before serving and garnish with orange zest.

Nutritional Value (Amount per Serving):

Calories: 282; Fat: 7.86; Carb: 48.58; Protein: 5.63

Caramelized Onion and Bacon Quiche

Prep Time: 20 Minutes   Cook Time: 4 Hours   Serves: 6

Ingredients:

- 1 gluten-free pie crust
- 6 large eggs, beaten
- 1 cup cooked and crumbled bacon
- 1 cup caramelized onions
- 1 cup dairy-free shredded cheese
- 1 cup unsweetened almond milk
- 1 teaspoon dried thyme
- Salt and pepper to taste

Directions:

1. Grease the slow cooker with cooking spray.
2. Place the gluten-free pie crust in the slow cooker, covering the bottom and sides.
3. In a bowl, whisk together eggs, bacon, caramelized onions, dairy-free shredded cheese, almond milk, dried thyme, salt, and pepper.
4. Pour the mixture into the pie crust.
5. Cover and cook on low for 4 hours or until the quiche is set.
6. Slice and serve warm.

Nutritional Value (Amount per Serving):

Calories: 320; Fat: 20.24; Carb: 22.51; Protein: 13.64

Slow Cooker Quinoa Breakfast Bowl

Prep Time: 15 Minutes   Cook Time: 3 Hours   Serves: 4

Ingredients:

- 1 cup quinoa, rinsed

- 2 cups almond milk
- 1 apple, diced
- 1/4 cup raisins
- 1 teaspoon cinnamon
- 1/4 cup chopped nuts (e.g., almonds or walnuts)
- 2 tablespoons honey
- Fresh berries for garnish (optional)

Directions:

1. Rinse the quinoa under cold water and drain.
2. In the slow cooker, combine quinoa, almond milk, diced apple, raisins, and cinnamon.
3. Stir the mixture well, cover, and cook on low for 3 hours or until the quinoa is tender.
4. In the last 15 minutes of cooking, stir in the chopped nuts and drizzle honey over the top.
5. Once cooked, fluff the quinoa with a fork.
6. Serve the breakfast bowl warm, garnished with fresh berries if desired.

Nutritional Value (Amount per Serving):

Calories: 315; Fat: 7.71; Carb: 54.7; Protein: 9.25

Crock Pot Veggie Frittata

Prep Time: 20 Minutes   Cook Time: 2 Hours   Serves: 6

Ingredients:

- 8 eggs, beaten
- 1 cup diced bell peppers (mixed colors)
- 1 cup cherry tomatoes, halved
- 1/2 cup diced red onion
- 1 cup spinach, chopped
- 1 cup shredded dairy-free cheese
- Salt and pepper to taste
- Cooking spray

Directions:

1. Grease the slow cooker with cooking spray.
2. In a bowl, whisk together eggs, bell peppers, cherry tomatoes, red onion, spinach, dairy-free cheese, salt, and pepper.
3. Pour the mixture into the slow cooker.
4. Cover and cook on low for 2 hours or until the frittata is set in the center.
5. Slice and serve warm.

Nutritional Value (Amount per Serving):

Calories: 212; Fat: 12.92; Carb: 4.9; Protein: 18.52

Overnight Slow Cooker Steel-Cut Oats

Prep Time: 5 Minutes   Cook Time: 8 Hours   Serves: 6

Ingredients:

- 2 cups gluten-free steel-cut oats
- 6 cups water
- 1 cup unsweetened almond milk
- 1/4 cup maple syrup
- 1 teaspoon vanilla extract
- 1/2 teaspoon cinnamon
- Pinch of salt
- Toppings: sliced bananas, chopped nuts, and a drizzle of honey

Directions:

1. Combine steel-cut oats, water, almond milk, maple syrup, vanilla extract, cinnamon, and salt in the slow cooker.
2. Stir well, cover, and cook on low for 8 hours.
3. Before serving, stir the oats and add more almond milk if needed.
4. Serve topped with sliced bananas, chopped nuts, and a drizzle of honey.

Nutritional Value (Amount per Serving):

Calories: 150; Fat: 2.8; Carb: 37.75; Protein: 5.87

Cinnamon Raisin Slow Cooker French Toast

Prep Time: 20 Minutes   Cook Time: 3 Hours   Serves: 6

Ingredients:

- 1 loaf gluten-free bread, cubed
- 8 large eggs
- 2 cups almond milk
- 1/2 cup maple syrup
- 1 teaspoon vanilla extract
- 1 teaspoon ground cinnamon
- 1/2 cup raisins
- Powdered sugar for garnish (optional)

Directions:

1. Grease the slow cooker with cooking spray.
2. Place the cubed gluten-free bread in the slow cooker.
3. In a bowl, whisk together eggs, almond milk, maple syrup, vanilla extract, and cinnamon.
4. Pour the egg mixture over the bread, making sure all pieces are coated.
5. Sprinkle raisins over the top.
6. Cover and cook on low for 3 hours or until the French toast is set.
7. Sprinkle with powdered sugar before serving if desired.

Nutritional Value (Amount per Serving):

Calories: 202; Fat: 7.23; Carb: 29.69; Protein: 4.64

Slow Cooker Sweet Potato and Sausage Hash

Prep Time: 20 Minutes   Cook Time: 4 Hours   Serves: 6

Ingredients:

- 2 large sweet potatoes, peeled and diced
- 1 pound gluten-free sausage, crumbled
- 1 onion, finely chopped
- 1 red bell pepper, diced
- 1 green bell pepper, diced
- 2 cloves garlic, minced
- 1 teaspoon smoked paprika
- 1/2 teaspoon dried thyme
- Salt and pepper to taste
- 6 large eggs (optional, for serving)

Directions:

1. In a large skillet, brown the crumbled sausage over medium heat until cooked through. Drain excess fat.
2. In the slow cooker, combine sweet potatoes, cooked sausage, onion, bell peppers, garlic, smoked paprika, thyme, salt, and pepper.
3. Stir well to evenly distribute the ingredients.
4. Cover and cook on low for 4 hours or until the sweet potatoes are tender.
5. If desired, fry or poach eggs and serve them on top of the hash.
6. Serve warm and enjoy!

Nutritional Value (Amount per Serving):

Calories: 322; Fat: 18.45; Carb: 24.87; Protein: 18.68

Cranberry Orange Bread Pudding

Prep Time: 20 Minutes   Cook Time: 3 Hours   Serves: 8

Ingredients:

- 1 loaf gluten-free bread, cubed
- 1 cup fresh cranberries
- 4 large eggs, beaten
- 2 cups almond milk
- 1/2 cup honey or maple syrup
- 1 teaspoon orange zest
- 1/2 teaspoon ground cinnamon
- Pinch of salt
- Orange slices for garnish

Directions:

1. Grease the slow cooker with cooking spray.
2. Place the gluten-free bread cubes and fresh cranberries in the slow cooker.
3. In a bowl, whisk together beaten eggs, almond milk, honey or maple syrup, orange zest, ground cinnamon, and a pinch of salt.
4. Pour the egg mixture over the bread and cranberries.
5. Stir gently, cover, and cook on low for 3 hours or until the bread pudding is set.
6. Garnish with orange slices before serving.

Nutritional Value (Amount per Serving):

Calories: 139; Fat: 3.2; Carb: 26; Protein: 2.15

Crock Pot Greek Yogurt Parfait

Prep Time: 10 Minutes   Cook Time: 2 Hours   Serves: 4

Ingredients:

- 4 cups dairy-free Greek yogurt
- 1 cup gluten-free granola
- 1 cup mixed berries (strawberries, blueberries, raspberries)
- 1/4 cup honey or maple syrup
- 1/2 teaspoon vanilla extract
- Mint leaves for garnish

Directions:

1. In the slow cooker, heat dairy-free Greek yogurt on low for 2 hours or until warmed.
2. In serving glasses or bowls, layer warm yogurt, gluten-free granola, mixed berries, honey or maple syrup, and vanilla extract.
3. Repeat the layers.
4. Chill in the refrigerator for at least 1 hour before serving.
5. Garnish with mint leaves.

Nutritional Value (Amount per Serving):

Calories: 307; Fat: 11.7; Carb: 41.42; Protein: 10.44

Overnight Slow Cooker Apple Cinnamon French Toast

Prep Time: 20 Minutes   Cook Time: 8 Hours   Serves: 8

Ingredients:

- 1 loaf gluten-free bread, cubed
- 8 eggs, beaten

- 2 cups almond milk
- 1/2 cup unsweetened applesauce
- 1/4 cup maple syrup
- 1 teaspoon ground cinnamon
- 1/2 teaspoon vanilla extract
- 2 apples, peeled and sliced
- 1/2 cup chopped pecans

Directions:

1. Grease the slow cooker with cooking spray.
2. Place the gluten-free bread cubes in the slow cooker.
3. In a bowl, whisk together beaten eggs, almond milk, applesauce, maple syrup, ground cinnamon, and vanilla extract.
4. Pour the egg mixture over the bread cubes.
5. Add sliced apples and chopped pecans on top.
6. Cover and refrigerate overnight.
7. Cook on low for 8 hours or until the French toast is set.
8. Serve warm.

Nutritional Value (Amount per Serving):

Calories: 271; Fat: 15.09; Carb: 24.56; Protein: 10.46

Slow Cooker Breakfast Enchiladas

Prep Time: 20 Minutes   Cook Time: 4 Hours   Serves: 6

Ingredients:

- 1 pound ground turkey or chicken
- 1 onion, finely chopped
- 1 bell pepper, diced
- 1 can (14 oz) black beans, drained and rinsed
- 1 cup salsa
- 1 teaspoon ground cumin
- 1/2 teaspoon chili powder
- Salt and pepper to taste
- 6 gluten-free tortillas
- 1 cup dairy-free shredded cheese
- Fresh cilantro for garnish

Directions:

1. In a skillet, brown the ground turkey or chicken until cooked through. Drain excess fat.
2. In the slow cooker, combine cooked meat, chopped onion, diced bell pepper, black beans, salsa, cumin, chili powder, salt, and pepper.
3. Stir well, then fill gluten-free tortillas with the mixture and place them in the slow cooker.
4. Sprinkle dairy-free shredded cheese on top.

5. Cover and cook on low for 4 hours or until the enchiladas are heated through.
6. Garnish with fresh cilantro before serving.

Nutritional Value (Amount per Serving):

Calories: 391; Fat: 9.14; Carb: 46.72; Protein: 31.69

Lemon Poppy Seed Quinoa Pancakes

Prep Time: 15 Minutes   Cook Time: 2 Hours   Serves: 4

Ingredients:

- 1 cup quinoa flour
- 1/2 cup almond flour
- 2 tablespoons poppy seeds
- 1 teaspoon baking powder
- 1/2 teaspoon baking soda
- Pinch of salt
- 1 cup unsweetened almond milk

- 2 tablespoons lemon juice
- 2 tablespoons maple syrup
- 2 large eggs
- 1 teaspoon vanilla extract
- Zest of 1 lemon
- Cooking spray

Directions:

1. In a bowl, whisk together quinoa flour, almond flour, poppy seeds, baking powder, baking soda, and a pinch of salt.
2. In another bowl, whisk together almond milk, lemon juice, maple syrup, eggs, vanilla extract, and lemon zest.
3. Combine wet and dry ingredients and mix until well combined.
4. Grease the slow cooker with cooking spray and pour in the pancake batter.
5. Cover and cook on low for 2 hours or until the pancakes are set.
6. Serve with your favorite toppings.

Nutritional Value (Amount per Serving):

Calories: 279; Fat: 7.59; Carb: 44.66; Protein: 8.9

Chapter 2: Meat and Poultry

Cranberry Orange Slow Cooker Turkey Breast

Prep Time: 15 Minutes   Cook Time: 6 Hours   Serves: 8

Ingredients:

- 4 pounds bone-in turkey breast
- 1 cup cranberry sauce (gluten-free)
- 1/2 cup orange juice
- 1/4 cup maple syrup
- 2 tablespoons Dijon mustard
- 1 teaspoon dried thyme
- Salt and pepper to taste
- Fresh cranberries for garnish (optional)

Directions:

1. Place the turkey breast in the slow cooker.
2. In a bowl, whisk together cranberry sauce, orange juice, maple syrup, Dijon mustard, dried thyme, salt, and pepper.
3. Pour the mixture over the turkey.
4. Cook on low for 6 hours.
5. Baste the turkey with the juices halfway through.
6. Garnish with fresh cranberries before serving.

Nutritional Value (Amount per Serving):

Calories: 427; Fat: 4.94; Carb: 23.5; Protein: 68.78

Slow Cooker Balsamic Glazed Chicken

Prep Time: 15 Minutes   Cook Time: 4 Hours   Serves: 6

Ingredients:

- 4 boneless, skinless chicken breasts
- 1 cup balsamic vinegar
- 1/2 cup honey
- 1/4 cup gluten-free soy sauce
- 4 cloves garlic, minced
- 1 teaspoon dried thyme
- Salt and pepper to taste
- 2 tablespoons cornstarch (for thickening)

Directions:

1. Season chicken breasts with salt and pepper and place them in the slow cooker.
2. In a bowl, whisk together balsamic vinegar, honey, gluten-free soy sauce,

garlic, and thyme.

3. Pour the mixture over the chicken, ensuring it is well-coated.
4. Cook on low for 4 hours.
5. In the last 30 minutes, mix cornstarch with a little water and add it to the slow cooker for a thicker glaze.
6. Serve the chicken over cooked rice or quinoa.

Nutritional Value (Amount per Serving):

Calories: 409; Fat: 8.66; Carb: 66.53; Protein: 15.56

Slow Cooker Turkey Chili

Prep Time: 15 Minutes   Cook Time: 6 Hours   Serves: 6

Ingredients:

- 1 pound ground turkey
- 1 onion, diced
- 2 bell peppers, diced
- 3 cloves garlic, minced
- 1 can (15 oz) gluten-free black beans, drained and rinsed
- 1 can (15 oz) gluten-free kidney beans, drained and rinsed
- 1 can (28 oz) crushed tomatoes
- 2 tablespoons chili powder
- 1 tablespoon cumin
- Salt and pepper to taste

Directions:

1. In a skillet, brown the ground turkey over medium heat. Drain excess fat.
2. Transfer the turkey to the slow cooker and add diced onion, bell peppers, garlic, black beans, kidney beans, crushed tomatoes, chili powder, cumin, salt, and pepper.
3. Stir well, cover, and cook on low for 6 hours.
4. Adjust seasoning before serving. Serve with gluten-free cornbread.

Nutritional Value (Amount per Serving):

Calories: 239; Fat: 9.86; Carb: 18.87; Protein: 20.65

Honey Garlic Slow Cooker Chicken Thighs

Prep Time: 10 Minutes   Cook Time: 5 Hours   Serves: 4

Ingredients:

- 8 bone-in, skin-on chicken thighs

- 1/2 cup gluten-free soy sauce
- 1/2 cup honey
- 1/4 cup ketchup
- 2 cloves garlic, minced
- 1 teaspoon dried basil
- 1/2 teaspoon red pepper flakes (optional)

Directions:

1. Place chicken thighs in the slow cooker.
2. In a bowl, whisk together soy sauce, honey, ketchup, garlic, basil, and red pepper flakes.
3. Pour the sauce over the chicken.
4. Cook on low for 5 hours.
5. Serve the chicken over rice, spooning the sauce on top.

Nutritional Value (Amount per Serving):

Calories: 1163; Fat: 100.44; Carb: 43.2; Protein: 25.03

Lemon Herb Slow Cooker Chicken Thighs

Prep Time: 15 Minutes   Cook Time: 6 Hours   Serves: 5

Ingredients:

- 8 bone-in, skin-on chicken thighs
- 1/4 cup olive oil
- Juice of 2 lemons
- 3 cloves garlic, minced
- 1 tablespoon dried oregano
- 1 tablespoon dried rosemary
- Salt and pepper to taste
- Fresh parsley for garnish

Directions:

1. In a bowl, whisk together olive oil, lemon juice, minced garlic, oregano, rosemary, salt, and pepper.
2. Place chicken thighs in the slow cooker and pour the lemon herb mixture over them.
3. Ensure the chicken is well coated, then cook on low for 6 hours.
4. Garnish with fresh parsley before serving. Serve with roasted vegetables or rice.

Nutritional Value (Amount per Serving):

Calories: 908; Fat: 91.2; Carb: 4.88; Protein: 17.96

Mango Coconut Curry Chicken

Prep Time: 20 Minutes   Cook Time: 5 Hours   Serves: 6

Ingredients:

- 2 pounds boneless, skinless chicken breasts, cut into cubes
- 1 large mango, peeled, pitted, and diced
- 1 can (14 oz) coconut milk
- 1 onion, finely chopped
- 3 cloves garlic, minced
- 1 red bell pepper, sliced
- 2 tablespoons gluten-free curry powder
- 1 teaspoon ground coriander
- 1 teaspoon ground cumin
- 1/2 teaspoon turmeric
- Salt and pepper to taste
- Fresh cilantro for garnish
- Cooked gluten-free rice for serving

Directions:

1. In the slow cooker, combine chicken cubes, diced mango, coconut milk, chopped onion, minced garlic, and sliced red bell pepper.
2. In a small bowl, mix curry powder, ground coriander, cumin, turmeric, salt, and pepper. Sprinkle the spice mixture over the chicken and stir to coat evenly.
3. Cook on low for 5 hours or until the chicken is tender and cooked through.
4. Serve the curry chicken over cooked gluten-free rice.
5. Garnish with fresh cilantro before serving.

Nutritional Value (Amount per Serving):

Calories: 460; Fat: 24.99; Carb: 45.13; Protein: 16.86

Buffalo Chicken Lettuce Wraps

Prep Time: 15 Minutes   Cook Time: 4 Hours   Serves: 6

Ingredients:

- 2 pounds boneless, skinless chicken breasts
- 1 cup gluten-free buffalo sauce
- 1/4 cup chicken broth
- 1 teaspoon garlic powder
- 1 teaspoon onion powder
- 1 teaspoon dried dill
- 1 head iceberg lettuce, leaves separated
- Blue cheese crumbles for topping (optional)
- Chopped celery for garnish

Directions:

1. Place chicken breasts in the slow cooker.
2. In a bowl, mix buffalo sauce, chicken broth, garlic powder, onion powder, and dried dill.
3. Pour the mixture over the chicken.

4. Cook on low for 4 hours.
5. Shred the chicken and serve in lettuce leaves.
6. Top with blue cheese crumbles and chopped celery.

Nutritional Value (Amount per Serving):

Calories: 446; Fat: 14.7; Carb: 56.82; Protein: 21.68

Honey Mustard Glazed Chicken Thighs

Prep Time: 10 Minutes   Cook Time: 5 Hours   Serves: 4

Ingredients:

- 8 bone-in, skin-on chicken thighs
- 1/3 cup gluten-free Dijon mustard
- 1/4 cup honey
- 2 tablespoons gluten-free soy sauce
- 2 cloves garlic, minced
- 1 teaspoon dried thyme
- Salt and pepper to taste

Directions:

1. Place chicken thighs in the slow cooker.
2. In a bowl, whisk together Dijon mustard, honey, soy sauce, minced garlic, dried thyme, salt, and pepper.
3. Pour the mixture over the chicken.
4. Cook on low for 5 hours.
5. Baste the chicken with the glaze during cooking.
6. Serve the chicken thighs over quinoa or rice.

Nutritional Value (Amount per Serving):

Calories: 968; Fat: 89.2; Carb: 22.25; Protein: 20.97

Lime Cilantro Slow Cooker Chicken Tacos

Prep Time: 15 Minutes   Cook Time: 6 Hours   Serves: 6

Ingredients:

- 2 pounds boneless, skinless chicken thighs
- Juice of 3 limes
- 1/4 cup chopped fresh cilantro
- 2 teaspoons ground cumin
- 1 teaspoon chili powder
- 1 teaspoon garlic powder
- Salt and pepper to taste
- Corn tortillas for serving
- Salsa, guacamole, and shredded lettuce for toppings

Directions:

1. Place chicken thighs in the slow cooker.
2. In a bowl, mix lime juice, chopped cilantro, cumin, chili powder, garlic powder, salt, and pepper.
3. Pour the mixture over the chicken.
4. Cook on low for 6 hours.
5. Shred the chicken and serve in corn tortillas with your favorite toppings.

Nutritional Value (Amount per Serving):

Calories: 401; Fat: 10.46; Carb: 60.19; Protein: 17.79

Mushroom and Spinach Stuffed Turkey Breast

Prep Time: 20 Minutes   Cook Time: 5 Hours   Serves: 6

Ingredients:

- 3 pounds boneless turkey breast
- 1 cup fresh spinach, chopped
- 1 cup mushrooms, finely chopped
- 1/2 cup grated Parmesan cheese
- 2 cloves garlic, minced
- 1 teaspoon dried thyme
- Salt and pepper to taste
- 1 cup gluten-free chicken broth
- 2 tablespoons olive oil

Directions:

1. Butterfly the turkey breast and pound it to an even thickness.
2. In a bowl, combine chopped spinach, mushrooms, Parmesan cheese, minced garlic, dried thyme, salt, and pepper.
3. Spread the mixture over the turkey breast and roll it up, securing with kitchen twine.
4. In a skillet, heat olive oil over medium-high heat. Brown the turkey on all sides.
5. Transfer the turkey to the slow cooker and pour chicken broth over it.
6. Cook on low for 5 hours. Slice and serve.

Nutritional Value (Amount per Serving):

Calories: 420; Fat: 11.72; Carb: 3.12; Protein: 71.83

Teriyaki Pineapple Chicken

Prep Time: 15 Minutes   Cook Time: 4 Hours   Serves: 4

Ingredients:

- 4 boneless, skinless chicken breasts
- 1 cup gluten-free teriyaki sauce

- 1 can (20 oz) pineapple chunks, drained
- 1 red bell pepper, sliced
- 1 onion, sliced
- 2 tablespoons gluten-free cornstarch
- 2 tablespoons water
- Sesame seeds for garnish
- Cooked rice for serving

Directions:

1. Place chicken breasts in the slow cooker.
2. Pour teriyaki sauce over the chicken and add pineapple chunks, sliced red bell pepper, and sliced onion.
3. Cook on low for 4 hours.
4. In the last 30 minutes, mix cornstarch with water and add it to the slow cooker for a thicker sauce.
5. Serve over cooked rice, garnished with sesame seeds.

Nutritional Value (Amount per Serving):

Calories: 502; Fat: 12.78; Carb: 72.44; Protein: 23.74

Rosemary Lemon Butter Crock Pot Chicken

Prep Time: 15 Minutes   Cook Time: 5 Hours   Serves: 4

Ingredients:

- 4 bone-in, skin-on chicken thighs
- 1/4 cup butter, melted
- Juice of 1 lemon
- 2 tablespoons fresh rosemary, chopped
- 3 cloves garlic, minced
- Salt and pepper to taste
- 1 cup gluten-free chicken broth
- 1/2 cup dry white wine (optional)

Directions:

1. Place chicken thighs in the slow cooker.
2. In a bowl, whisk together melted butter, lemon juice, chopped rosemary, minced garlic, salt, and pepper.
3. Pour the mixture over the chicken.
4. Add chicken broth and wine (if using) to the slow cooker.
5. Cook on low for 5 hours.
6. Serve the chicken with the flavorful juices.

Nutritional Value (Amount per Serving):

Calories: 1037; Fat: 103.17; Carb: 4.92; Protein: 23.09

Sesame Ginger Chicken Stir-Fry

Prep Time: 20 Minutes   Cook Time: 4 Hours   Serves: 6

Ingredients:

- 2 pounds boneless, skinless chicken breasts, cut into strips
- 1 cup gluten-free soy sauce
- 1/4 cup honey
- 2 tablespoons sesame oil
- 3 cloves garlic, minced
- 1 tablespoon fresh ginger, grated
- 1 cup broccoli florets
- 1 red bell pepper, sliced
- 1 carrot, julienned
- 2 tablespoons gluten-free cornstarch
- 2 tablespoons water
- Sesame seeds and green onions for garnish
- Cooked rice or quinoa for serving

Directions:

1. In the slow cooker, combine chicken strips, soy sauce, honey, sesame oil, minced garlic, and grated ginger.
2. Add broccoli, red bell pepper, and julienned carrot to the slow cooker.
3. Cook on low for 4 hours.
4. In the last 30 minutes, mix cornstarch with water and add it to the slow cooker for a thicker sauce.
5. Serve the chicken stir-fry over cooked rice or quinoa.
6. Garnish with sesame seeds and chopped green onions.

Nutritional Value (Amount per Serving):

Calories: 411; Fat: 15.03; Carb: 51.36; Protein: 19.04

Lemon Garlic Butter Turkey Meatballs

Prep Time: 15 Minutes   Cook Time: 4 Hours   Serves: 6

Ingredients:

- 1.5 pounds ground turkey
- 1 cup gluten-free breadcrumbs
- 1/4 cup milk
- 2 cloves garlic, minced
- 1/4 cup fresh parsley, chopped
- Zest of 1 lemon

- 1/4 cup grated Parmesan cheese
- Salt and pepper to taste
- 1/2 cup chicken broth
- 1/4 cup unsalted butter, melted
- Juice of 1 lemon

Directions:

1. In a bowl, combine ground turkey, breadcrumbs, milk, minced garlic, chopped parsley, lemon zest, Parmesan cheese, salt, and pepper. Form into meatballs.
2. Place meatballs in the slow cooker.
3. Mix chicken broth, melted butter, and lemon juice. Pour over the meatballs.
4. Cook on low for 4 hours.
5. Serve the turkey meatballs over gluten-free pasta or with a side of vegetables.

Nutritional Value (Amount per Serving):

Calories: 297; Fat: 16.9; Carb: 7.64; Protein: 29.16

Chapter 3: Beef, Pork and Lamb

Teriyaki Pineapple Pork

Prep Time: 15 Minutes   Cook Time: 6 Hours   Serves: 4

Ingredients:

- 2 lbs pork loin, sliced
- 1 cup gluten-free teriyaki sauce
- 1 can (20 oz) pineapple chunks, drained
- 1/4 cup honey
- 3 cloves garlic, minced
- 1 tablespoon grated ginger
- 2 tablespoons gluten-free soy sauce

Directions:

1. Place pork slices in the slow cooker.
2. In a bowl, mix teriyaki sauce, pineapple chunks, honey, garlic, ginger, and soy sauce.
3. Pour the mixture over the pork.
4. Cook on low for 6 hours. Serve over rice.

Nutritional Value (Amount per Serving):

Calories: 664; Fat: 25.2; Carb: 43.69; Protein: 63.47

Crock Pot Pulled Pork Tacos

Prep Time: 20 Minutes   Cook Time: 8 Hours   Serves: 8

Ingredients:

- 4 pounds pork shoulder, trimmed
- 1 cup gluten-free barbecue sauce
- 1/2 cup apple cider vinegar
- 1/4 cup brown sugar
- 1 tablespoon smoked paprika
- 2 teaspoons garlic powder
- 1 teaspoon cumin
- Corn tortillas (for serving)

Directions:

1. Place the pork shoulder in the slow cooker.
2. In a bowl, mix together barbecue sauce, apple cider vinegar, brown sugar, smoked paprika, garlic powder, and cumin.
3. Pour the sauce over the pork, making sure it's evenly coated.
4. Cook on low for 8 hours.
5. Shred the pork using two forks and mix it with the cooking juices.
6. Serve the pulled pork in corn tortillas with your favorite toppings.

Nutritional Value (Amount per Serving):

Calories: 690; Fat: 40.49; Carb: 17.87; Protein: 59.65

Gluten-Free Beef Stew

Prep Time: 20 Minutes   Cook Time: 8 Hours   Serves: 6

Ingredients:

- 2 pounds beef stew meat, cubed
- 4 cups gluten-free beef broth
- 1 cup baby carrots
- 1 cup celery, chopped
- 1 onion, diced
- 3 cloves garlic, minced
- 2 potatoes, peeled and diced
- 1 cup gluten-free frozen peas
- 2 teaspoons dried thyme
- Salt and pepper to taste
- 1/4 cup gluten-free all-purpose flour (for coating beef)

Directions:

1. Toss beef cubes in gluten-free flour to coat.
2. Brown the beef in a skillet over medium-high heat.
3. Transfer beef to the slow cooker and add beef broth, carrots, celery, onion, garlic, potatoes, thyme, salt, and pepper.
4. Cook on low for 8 hours.
5. In the last 30 minutes, add frozen peas.
6. Adjust seasoning before serving.

Nutritional Value (Amount per Serving):

Calories: 314; Fat: 13.09; Carb: 45.2; Protein: 5.04

Slow Cooker BBQ Meatballs

Prep Time: 20 Minutes   Cook Time: 4 Hours   Serves: 8

Ingredients:

- 1.5 pounds ground beef
- 1/2 cup gluten-free breadcrumbs
- 1/4 cup milk
- 2 cloves garlic, minced
- 1 egg
- Salt and pepper to taste
- 1 cup gluten-free barbecue sauce
- 1/4 cup honey
- 2 tablespoons apple cider vinegar
- 1 teaspoon smoked paprika

Directions:

1. In a bowl, combine ground beef, gluten-free breadcrumbs, milk, minced garlic, egg, salt, and pepper. Form into meatballs.
2. Brown meatballs in a skillet over medium heat.

3. Transfer meatballs to the slow cooker.
4. In a separate bowl, mix barbecue sauce, honey, apple cider vinegar, and smoked paprika. Pour over the meatballs.
5. Cook on low for 4 hours, ensuring meatballs are cooked through.
6. Serve meatballs as an appetizer or with gluten-free pasta.

Nutritional Value (Amount per Serving):

Calories: 314; Fat: 15.31; Carb: 17.75; Protein: 25.35

Lamb and Vegetable Curry

Prep Time: 15 Minutes   Cook Time: 7 Hours   Serves: 4

Ingredients:

- 2 lbs lamb stew meat, cubed
- 1 large onion, chopped
- 3 cloves garlic, minced
- 2 tablespoons gluten-free curry powder
- 1 teaspoon ground cumin
- 1 teaspoon ground coriander
- 1 can (14 oz) diced tomatoes
- 1 cup gluten-free chicken broth
- 1 cup green beans, trimmed
- Salt and pepper to taste
- Fresh cilantro for garnish

Directions:

1. In the slow cooker, combine lamb, onion, garlic, curry powder, cumin, coriander, tomatoes, and chicken broth.
2. Cook on low for 6 hours.
3. Add green beans, salt, and pepper. Cook for an additional hour.
4. Garnish with fresh cilantro before serving.

Nutritional Value (Amount per Serving):

Calories: 333; Fat: 20.55; Carb: 11.14; Protein: 26.27

Gluten-Free BBQ Beef Ribs

Prep Time: 20 Minutes   Cook Time: 7 Hours   Serves: 5

Ingredients:

- 3 lbs beef ribs
- 1 cup gluten-free barbecue sauce
- 1/4 cup brown sugar
- 1 teaspoon smoked paprika
- 1 teaspoon garlic powder
- 1 teaspoon onion powder
- Salt and pepper to taste

Directions:

1. Mix brown sugar, smoked paprika, garlic powder, onion powder, salt, and pepper in a bowl.

2. Rub the spice mixture evenly over the beef ribs.
3. Place the ribs in the slow cooker and pour barbecue sauce over them.
4. Cover and cook on low for 7 hours or until the meat is tender.

Nutritional Value (Amount per Serving):

Calories: 1016; Fat: 81.45; Carb: 24.13; Protein: 46.69

Mediterranean Lamb Stew

Prep Time: 20 Minutes   Cook Time: 8 Hours   Serves: 6

Ingredients:

- 2 lbs lamb stew meat, cubed
- 1 cup gluten-free chicken broth
- 1 can (14 oz) diced tomatoes
- 1 cup kalamata olives, pitted
- 1 cup artichoke hearts, quartered
- 1 red onion, chopped
- 3 cloves garlic, minced
- 1 teaspoon dried oregano
- 1 teaspoon dried rosemary
- Salt and pepper to taste

Directions:

1. Combine lamb, chicken broth, diced tomatoes, olives, artichoke hearts, red onion, garlic, oregano, rosemary, salt, and pepper in the slow cooker.
2. Cook on low for 8 hours or until lamb is tender.
3. Serve over quinoa or gluten-free couscous.

Nutritional Value (Amount per Serving):

Calories: 240; Fat: 15.65; Carb: 7.76; Protein: 17.79

Tangy Mango Pork Chops

Prep Time: 15 Minutes   Cook Time: 6 Hours   Serves: 4

Ingredients:

- 4 pork chops
- 1 cup mango, diced
- 1/4 cup gluten-free Dijon mustard
- 2 tablespoons maple syrup
- 1 tablespoon olive oil
- 1 teaspoon gluten-free soy sauce
- 1 teaspoon dried rosemary
- Salt and pepper to taste

Directions:

1. Season pork chops with salt and pepper.
2. In a bowl, mix mango, Dijon mustard, maple syrup, olive oil, soy sauce, and rosemary.
3. Place pork chops in the slow cooker and pour the mango mixture over them.
4. Cook on low for 6 hours.

Nutritional Value (Amount per Serving):

Calories: 423; Fat: 21.46; Carb: 14.95; Protein: 41.47

Lemon Herb Lamb Chops

Prep Time: 15 Minutes   Cook Time: 4 Hours   Serves: 4

Ingredients:

- 8 lamb chops
- 1/4 cup olive oil
- 2 tablespoons lemon juice
- 2 teaspoons dried rosemary
- 1 teaspoon dried thyme
- 3 cloves garlic, minced
- Salt and pepper to taste

Directions:

1. Season lamb chops with salt and pepper.
2. In a bowl, whisk together olive oil, lemon juice, rosemary, thyme, and garlic.
3. Place lamb chops in the slow cooker and pour the lemon herb mixture over them.
4. Cook on low for 4 hours.

Nutritional Value (Amount per Serving):

Calories: 1418; Fat: 75.99; Carb: 2.46; Protein: 181.68

Mexican Beef Chili

Prep Time: 20 Minutes   Cook Time: 7 Hours   Serves: 6

Ingredients:

- 2 lbs beef stew meat, cubed
- 1 onion, chopped
- 3 cloves garlic, minced
- 1 can (14 oz) diced tomatoes
- 1 can (15 oz) black beans, drained and rinsed
- 1 cup corn kernels
- 1 cup gluten-free beef broth
- 2 tablespoons chili powder
- 1 teaspoon cumin
- Salt and pepper to taste
- Shredded cheese and chopped green onions for topping

Directions:

1. In the slow cooker, combine beef, onion, garlic, diced tomatoes, black

beans, corn, beef broth, chili powder, cumin, salt, and pepper.

2. Cook on low for 7 hours.

3. Serve topped with shredded cheese and chopped green onions.

Nutritional Value (Amount per Serving):

Calories: 296; Fat: 14.11; Carb: 36.28; Protein: 9.16

Apple Cider Braised Pork Shoulder

Prep Time: 15 Minutes   Cook Time: 8 Hours   Serves: 6

Ingredients:

- 3 lbs pork shoulder, trimmed and cubed
- 2 cups gluten-free apple cider
- 1/4 cup maple syrup
- 1 tablespoon Dijon mustard
- 1 teaspoon dried sage
- 1 teaspoon cinnamon
- Salt and pepper to taste

Directions:

1. Season pork shoulder with salt and pepper.
2. In a bowl, mix apple cider, maple syrup, Dijon mustard, sage, and cinnamon.
3. Place pork shoulder in the slow cooker and pour the apple cider mixture over it.
4. Cook on low for 8 hours or until the pork is fork-tender.

Nutritional Value (Amount per Serving):

Calories: 684; Fat: 40.36; Carb: 19.43; Protein: 57.22

Crock Pot Beef and Broccoli

Prep Time: 15 Minutes   Cook Time: 4 Hours   Serves: 4

Ingredients:

- 1.5 lbs beef sirloin, thinly sliced
- 1 cup gluten-free beef broth
- 1/2 cup gluten-free soy sauce
- 1/3 cup honey
- 3 cloves garlic, minced
- 1 teaspoon ginger, grated
- 1 tablespoon sesame oil
- 2 tablespoons cornstarch
- 2 cups broccoli florets
- Sesame seeds for garnish
- Sliced green onions for garnish

Directions:

1. In a bowl, mix beef broth, soy sauce, honey, garlic, ginger, sesame oil, and

cornstarch.

2. Place sliced beef and broccoli in the slow cooker.
3. Pour the sauce over the beef and broccoli.
4. Cook on low for 4 hours. Serve over rice, garnished with sesame seeds and green onions.

Nutritional Value (Amount per Serving):

Calories: 514; Fat: 23.83; Carb: 35.52; Protein: 39.74

Mediterranean Pork and Chickpea Stew

Prep Time: 20 Minutes   Cook Time: 8 Hours   Serves: 6

Ingredients:

- 2 lbs pork shoulder, trimmed and cubed
- 1 can (14 oz) chickpeas, drained and rinsed
- 1 cup gluten-free chicken broth
- 1 cup cherry tomatoes, halved
- 1/2 cup Kalamata olives, pitted
- 1 red onion, chopped
- 3 cloves garlic, minced
- 1 teaspoon dried oregano
- 1 teaspoon dried rosemary
- Salt and pepper to taste

Directions:

1. Combine pork, chickpeas, chicken broth, cherry tomatoes, olives, red onion, garlic, oregano, rosemary, salt, and pepper in the slow cooker.
2. Cook on low for 8 hours or until the pork is tender.
3. Serve over quinoa or gluten-free couscous.

Nutritional Value (Amount per Serving):

Calories: 488; Fat: 29.16; Carb: 13.02; Protein: 41.74

Cranberry Balsamic Glazed Beef

Prep Time: 15 Minutes   Cook Time: 7 Hours   Serves: 5

Ingredients:

- 3 lbs beef chuck roast
- 1 cup cranberry juice
- 1/4 cup balsamic vinegar
- 1/4 cup honey
- 2 tablespoons gluten-free soy sauce
- 1 teaspoon dried thyme
- Salt and pepper to taste

Directions:

1. Place beef chuck roast in the slow cooker.
2. In a bowl, mix cranberry juice, balsamic vinegar, honey, soy sauce, thyme, salt, and pepper.
3. Pour the mixture over the beef.
4. Cook on low for 7 hours or until the beef is tender.

Nutritional Value (Amount per Serving):

Calories: 595; Fat: 23.11; Carb: 24.2; Protein: 73.35

Spicy Orange Glazed Pork Chops

Prep Time: 15 Minutes   Cook Time: 5 Hours   Serves: 4

Ingredients:

- 4 pork chops
- 1/2 cup orange juice
- 1/4 cup gluten-free soy sauce
- 2 tablespoons honey
- 1 tablespoon Sriracha sauce
- 2 cloves garlic, minced
- 1 teaspoon grated ginger
- Sesame seeds for garnish
- Sliced green onions for garnish

Directions:

1. Season pork chops with salt and pepper.
2. In a bowl, whisk together orange juice, soy sauce, honey, Sriracha sauce, garlic, and ginger.
3. Place pork chops in the slow cooker and pour the orange glaze over them.
4. Cook on low for 5 hours. Garnish with sesame seeds and sliced green onions before serving.

Nutritional Value (Amount per Serving):

Calories: 402; Fat: 18.69; Carb: 14.47; Protein: 42.5

Lamb and Vegetable Tagine

Prep Time: 20 Minutes   Cook Time: 8 Hours   Serves: 6

Ingredients:

- 2 lbs lamb stew meat, cubed
- 1 large sweet potato, peeled and diced
- 1 cup baby carrots, sliced
- 1 cup dried apricots, halved
- 1 onion, chopped
- 3 cloves garlic, minced

- 1 teaspoon ground cumin
- 1 teaspoon ground coriander
- 1 teaspoon ground cinnamon
- 1 can (14 oz) gluten-free chicken broth
- Salt and pepper to taste

Directions:

1. In the slow cooker, combine lamb, sweet potato, carrots, apricots, onion, garlic, cumin, coriander, cinnamon, chicken broth, salt, and pepper.
2. Cook on low for 8 hours. Serve over gluten-free couscous.

Nutritional Value (Amount per Serving):

Calories: 283; Fat: 13.39; Carb: 23.64; Protein: 18.02

Pineapple Coconut Pork Curry

Prep Time: 20 Minutes   Cook Time: 7 Hours   Serves: 4

Ingredients:

- 2 lbs pork loin, cubed
- 1 can (14 oz) coconut milk
- 1 cup pineapple chunks
- 1 onion, chopped
- 3 cloves garlic, minced
- 2 tablespoons gluten-free yellow curry paste
- 1 teaspoon ground turmeric
- 1 teaspoon ground coriander
- 1 teaspoon fish sauce (optional)
- Salt and pepper to taste
- Fresh cilantro for garnish

Directions:

1. In the slow cooker, combine pork, coconut milk, pineapple chunks, onion, garlic, curry paste, turmeric, coriander, fish sauce, salt, and pepper.
2. Cook on low for 7 hours. Garnish with fresh cilantro before serving.

Nutritional Value (Amount per Serving):

Calories: 787; Fat: 49.33; Carb: 25.8; Protein: 61.88

Chapter 4: Fish and Seafood

Crock Pot Garlic Butter Shrimp Scampi

Prep Time: 15 Minutes   Cook Time: 2 Hours   Serves: 4

Ingredients:

- 1.5 pounds large shrimp, peeled and deveined
- 1/2 cup unsalted butter, melted
- 4 cloves garlic, minced
- 1/4 cup fresh parsley, chopped
- 1 teaspoon red pepper flakes (optional)
- Salt and pepper to taste
- Zucchini noodles (zoodles) for serving

Directions:

1. In a bowl, combine shrimp, melted butter, garlic, parsley, red pepper flakes, salt, and pepper.
2. Transfer the mixture to the crock pot.
3. Cook on low for 2 hours, stirring occasionally.
4. Serve the garlic butter shrimp scampi over zucchini noodles.

Nutritional Value (Amount per Serving):

Calories: 224; Fat: 15.86; Carb: 17.36; Protein: 4.18

Slow-Cooked Lemon Garlic Shrimp

Prep Time: 15 Minutes   Cook Time: 2 Hours   Serves: 4-6

Ingredients:

- 1 pound large shrimp, peeled and deveined
- 4 cloves garlic, minced
- 1 lemon, juiced and zested
- 2 tablespoons olive oil
- 1 teaspoon dried oregano
- Salt and pepper to taste

Directions:

1. In a bowl, combine shrimp, minced garlic, lemon juice, lemon zest, olive oil, oregano, salt, and pepper.
2. Transfer the mixture to the crock pot.
3. Cook on low for 2 hours, stirring occasionally.
4. Serve the lemon garlic shrimp over rice or quinoa.

Nutritional Value (Amount per Serving):

Calories: 68; Fat: 5.61; Carb: 4.4; Protein: 0.92

Mediterranean Style Crock Pot Cod

Prep Time: 20 Minutes   Cook Time: 3 Hours   Serves: 4

Ingredients:

- 4 cod fillets
- 1 cup cherry tomatoes, halved
- 1/2 cup Kalamata olives, sliced
- 1/4 cup capers
- 3 cloves garlic, minced
- 1/4 cup fresh parsley, chopped

Directions:

1. Place cod fillets in the crock pot.
2. In a bowl, mix tomatoes, olives, capers, and garlic. Spoon over the cod.
3. Cover and cook on low for 3 hours.
4. Sprinkle with fresh parsley before serving.

Nutritional Value (Amount per Serving):

Calories: 107; Fat: 2.38; Carb: 2.71; Protein: 18.3

Coconut-Lime Crock Pot Salmon

Prep Time: 10 Minutes   Cook Time: 2 Hours 30 Minutes   Serves: 4

Ingredients:

- 4 salmon fillets
- 1 can (13.5 oz) coconut milk
- 2 limes, juiced and zested
- 2 tablespoons fresh cilantro, chopped
- 1 teaspoon ground cumin
- Salt and pepper to taste

Directions:

1. Place salmon fillets in the crock pot.
2. In a bowl, mix coconut milk, lime juice, lime zest, cilantro, cumin, salt, and pepper.
3. Pour the mixture over the salmon.
4. Cook on low for 2.5 hours, basting with the sauce occasionally.

Nutritional Value (Amount per Serving):

Calories: 319; Fat: 27.03; Carb: 8.47; Protein: 14.31

Spicy Cajun Crock Pot Catfish Stew

Prep Time: 15 Minutes   Cook Time: 4 Hours   Serves: 6

Ingredients:

- 1.5 pounds catfish fillets, cut into chunks
- 1 onion, diced

- 2 bell peppers, diced
- 3 celery stalks, sliced
- 1 can (14 oz) diced tomatoes
- 2 cloves garlic, minced
- 2 teaspoons Cajun seasoning
- 1 teaspoon dried thyme
- Salt and pepper to taste

Directions:

1. Combine catfish, onion, bell peppers, celery, diced tomatoes, garlic, Cajun seasoning, thyme, salt, and pepper in the crock pot.
2. Cook on low for 4 hours, stirring occasionally.
3. Serve the spicy Cajun catfish stew over rice or quinoa.

Nutritional Value (Amount per Serving):

Calories: 135; Fat: 3.36; Carb: 6.11; Protein: 19.65

Herb-Infused Crock Pot Scallops

Prep Time: 10 Minutes   Cook Time: 1 Hour 30 Minutes   Serves: 4

Ingredients:

- 1 pound scallops
- 1/4 cup olive oil
- 2 tablespoons fresh basil, chopped
- 2 tablespoons fresh chives, chopped
- 1 tablespoon fresh thyme leaves
- 2 cloves garlic, minced

Directions:

1. In a bowl, mix scallops, olive oil, basil, chives, thyme, and garlic.
2. Transfer the mixture to the crock pot.
3. Cook on low for 1.5 hours, stirring gently halfway through.
4. Serve the herb-infused scallops over a bed of steamed vegetables.

Nutritional Value (Amount per Serving):

Calories: 201; Fat: 14.09; Carb: 4.35; Protein: 13.9

Lemon Herb Crock Pot Tilapia

Prep Time: 10 Minutes   Cook Time: 2 Hours 30 Minutes   Serves: 4

Ingredients:

- 4 tilapia fillets
- 1 lemon, thinly sliced
- 2 tablespoons olive oil
- 1 teaspoon dried thyme
- 1 teaspoon dried rosemary
- Salt and pepper to taste

Directions:

1. Place tilapia fillets in the crock pot.
2. Drizzle with olive oil and sprinkle with thyme, rosemary, salt, and pepper.
3. Arrange lemon slices on top.
4. Cook on low for 2.5 hours, or until the tilapia is flaky.

Nutritional Value (Amount per Serving):

Calories: 179; Fat: 8.79; Carb: 1.98; Protein: 23.58

Tomato-Basil Crock Pot Cod Stew

Prep Time: 20 Minutes   Cook Time: 3 Hours   Serves: 6

Ingredients:

- 1.5 pounds cod fillets, cut into chunks
- 1 onion, diced
- 2 carrots, sliced
- 3 cloves garlic, minced
- 1 can (14 oz) diced tomatoes
- 1/4 cup fresh basil, chopped
- 1 teaspoon dried oregano
- Salt and pepper to taste

Directions

1. Combine cod, onion, carrots, garlic, diced tomatoes, basil, oregano, salt, and pepper in the crock pot.
2. Cook on low for 3 hours, stirring occasionally.
3. Serve the tomato-basil cod stew with gluten-free bread.

Nutritional Value (Amount per Serving):

Calories: 97; Fat: 0.6; Carb: 4.25; Protein: 18.07

Thai Coconut Crock Pot Shrimp Curry

Prep Time: 20 Minutes   Cook Time: 3 Hours   Serves: 4

Ingredients:

- 1.5 pounds large shrimp, peeled and deveined
- 1 can (13.5 oz) coconut milk
- 2 tablespoons red curry paste
- 1 tablespoon fish sauce
- 1 tablespoon brown sugar
- 1 red bell pepper, sliced
- 1 cup snap peas
- Cooked rice for serving

Directions:

1. In a bowl, mix shrimp, coconut milk, red curry paste, fish sauce, and brown

sugar.

2. Transfer the mixture to the crock pot and add red bell pepper and snap peas.
3. Cook on low for 3 hours, stirring occasionally.
4. Serve the Thai coconut shrimp curry over cooked rice.

Nutritional Value (Amount per Serving):

Calories: 289; Fat: 23.62; Carb: 20.07; Protein: 4.15

Smoky Paprika Crock Pot Salmon

Prep Time: 15 Minutes   Cook Time: 2 Hours   Serves: 4

Ingredients:

- 4 salmon fillets
- 2 teaspoons smoked paprika
- 1 teaspoon garlic powder
- 1 teaspoon onion powder
- 1/2 teaspoon cayenne pepper (adjust to taste)
- 1/4 cup olive oil
- Lemon wedges for serving

Directions:

1. Rub salmon fillets with smoked paprika, garlic powder, onion powder, and cayenne pepper.
2. Drizzle olive oil in the crock pot.
3. Place salmon fillets in the crock pot.
4. Cook on low for 2 hours or until salmon flakes easily.
5. Serve the smoky paprika salmon with lemon wedges.

Nutritional Value (Amount per Serving):

Calories: 437; Fat: 28.07; Carb: 2.61; Protein: 41.68

Cilantro Lime Crock Pot Shrimp Tacos

Prep Time: 15 Minutes   Cook Time: 2 Hours 30 Minutes   Serves: 4

Ingredients:

- 1.5 pounds large shrimp, peeled and deveined
- 1/4 cup fresh cilantro, chopped
- 2 limes, juiced and zested
- 1 teaspoon ground cumin
- 1 teaspoon chili powder

- 1/2 teaspoon garlic powder
- Corn or gluten-free tortillas for serving

1. In a bowl, mix shrimp, cilantro, lime juice, lime zest, cumin, chili powder, and garlic powder.
2. Transfer the mixture to the crock pot.
3. Cook on low for 2.5 hours, stirring occasionally.
4. Serve the cilantro lime shrimp in tacos.

Calories: 91; Fat: 4.29; Carb: 10.92; Protein: 3.23

Herbed Crock Pot Clam Chowder

Prep Time: 20 Minutes   Cook Time: 3 Hours 30 Minutes   Serves: 6

- 2 cans (10 oz each) chopped clams, drained
- 4 cups potatoes, diced
- 1 onion, diced
- 2 celery stalks, sliced
- 3 cloves garlic, minced
- 2 teaspoons dried thyme
- 1 teaspoon dried dill
- 4 cups vegetable broth
- 2 cups non-dairy milk (such as almond or coconut)
- Salt and pepper to taste

1. In the crock pot, combine clams, potatoes, onion, celery, garlic, thyme, dill, vegetable broth, and non-dairy milk.
2. Cook on low for 3.5 hours or until potatoes are tender.
3. Season with salt and pepper before serving.

Calories: 161; Fat: 0.39; Carb: 37.99; Protein: 3.27

Mediterranean Crock Pot Swordfish

Prep Time: 15 Minutes   Cook Time: 3 Hours   Serves: 4

- 4 swordfish steaks
- 1 cup cherry tomatoes, halved

- 1/2 cup Kalamata olives, sliced
- 1/4 cup capers
- 2 tablespoons fresh oregano, chopped
- 2 tablespoons olive oil
- Salt and pepper to taste

Directions:

1. Place swordfish steaks in the crock pot.
2. In a bowl, mix cherry tomatoes, olives, capers, oregano, olive oil, salt, and pepper.
3. Spoon the mixture over the swordfish.
4. Cook on low for 3 hours, basting with the juices occasionally.

Nutritional Value (Amount per Serving):

Calories: 620; Fat: 41.99; Carb: 13.09; Protein: 48.26

Spicy Mango Crock Pot Shrimp

Prep Time: 15 Minutes   Cook Time: 2 Hours 30 Minutes   Serves: 4

Ingredients:

- 1.5 pounds large shrimp, peeled and deveined
- 1 ripe mango, peeled and diced
- 1/4 cup red onion, finely chopped
- 2 tablespoons fresh cilantro, chopped
- 1 jalapeño, seeded and minced
- 2 limes, juiced
- 1 teaspoon chili powder
- Salt and pepper to taste

Directions:

1. In a bowl, combine shrimp, mango, red onion, cilantro, jalapeño, lime juice, chili powder, salt, and pepper.
2. Transfer the mixture to the crock pot.
3. Cook on low for 2.5 hours, stirring occasionally.
4. Serve the spicy mango shrimp over rice.

Nutritional Value (Amount per Serving):

Calories: 61; Fat: 0.6; Carb: 13.9; Protein: 1.9

Honey Dijon Glazed Crock Pot Salmon

Prep Time: 15 Minutes   Cook Time: 2 Hours   Serves: 4

Ingredients:

- 4 salmon fillets
- 1/4 cup Dijon mustard

- 2 tablespoons honey
- 1 tablespoon soy sauce (gluten-free)
- 1 teaspoon minced garlic
- 1/2 teaspoon dried thyme
- Sesame seeds for garnish (optional)

Directions:

1. Place salmon fillets in the crock pot.
2. In a bowl, whisk together Dijon mustard, honey, soy sauce, garlic, and thyme.
3. Pour the sauce over the salmon.
4. Cook on low for 2 hours, basting with the sauce occasionally.
5. Garnish with sesame seeds before serving.

Nutritional Value (Amount per Serving):

Calories: 373; Fat: 16.81; Carb: 11.04; Protein: 42.62

Crock Pot Coconut-Lime Mahi Mahi

Prep Time: 15 Minutes   Cook Time: 3 Hours   Serves: 4

Ingredients:

- 4 mahi mahi fillets
- 1 can (13.5 oz) coconut milk
- 2 limes, juiced and zested
- 2 tablespoons fresh cilantro, chopped
- 1 tablespoon fish sauce
- 1 teaspoon ground coriander
- Salt and pepper to taste

Directions:

1. Place mahi mahi fillets in the crock pot.
2. In a bowl, mix coconut milk, lime juice, lime zest, cilantro, fish sauce, coriander, salt, and pepper.
3. Pour the mixture over the mahi mahi.
4. Cook on low for 3 hours, basting with the sauce occasionally.

Nutritional Value (Amount per Serving):

Calories: 478; Fat: 38.15; Carb: 16.05; Protein: 22.3

Mediterranean Crock Pot Octopus Stew

Prep Time: 20 Minutes   Cook Time: 4 Hours   Serves: 6

Ingredients:

- 2 pounds octopus, cleaned and chopped

- 1 onion, diced
- 2 bell peppers, diced
- 3 cloves garlic, minced
- 1 can (14 oz) crushed tomatoes
- 1/4 cup fresh parsley, chopped
- 2 teaspoons dried oregano
- 1 teaspoon smoked paprika
- Salt and pepper to taste

Directions:

1. In the crock pot, combine octopus, onion, bell peppers, garlic, crushed tomatoes, parsley, oregano, smoked paprika, salt, and pepper.
2. Cook on low for 4 hours, stirring occasionally.
3. Serve the Mediterranean octopus stew with crusty gluten-free bread.

Nutritional Value (Amount per Serving):

Calories: 150, Fat: 1.81; Carb: 9.36; Protein: 23.7

Crock Pot Sesame Ginger Glazed Tuna

Prep Time: 15 Minutes   Cook Time: 2 Hours   Serves: 4

Ingredients:

- 4 tuna steaks
- 1/4 cup gluten-free soy sauce
- 2 tablespoons sesame oil
- 2 tablespoons rice vinegar
- 1 tablespoon honey
- 1 tablespoon fresh ginger, grated
- 2 cloves garlic, minced
- Sesame seeds for garnish

Directions:

1. Place tuna steaks in the crock pot.
2. In a bowl, whisk together soy sauce, sesame oil, rice vinegar, honey, ginger, and garlic.
3. Pour the sauce over the tuna.
4. Cook on low for 2 hours, basting with the sauce occasionally.
5. Sprinkle with sesame seeds before serving.

Nutritional Value (Amount per Serving):

Calories: 597; Fat: 40.82; Carb: 6.28; Protein: 48.37

Chapter 5: Vegetables and Sides

Crock Pot Ratatouille

Prep Time: 20 Minutes   Cook Time: 4 Hours   Serves: 8

Ingredients:

- 1 eggplant, diced
- 2 zucchinis, sliced
- 1 bell pepper (any color), diced
- 1 onion, diced
- 3 cloves garlic, minced
- 1 can (14 oz) diced tomatoes, undrained
- 2 tbsp tomato paste
- 1 tsp dried thyme
- 1 tsp dried oregano
- Salt and pepper to taste
- Fresh basil for garnish

Directions:

1. Combine all vegetables, garlic, diced tomatoes, tomato paste, thyme, and oregano in the slow cooker.
2. Stir well, season with salt and pepper.
3. Cook on low for 4 hours or until vegetables are tender.
4. Garnish with fresh basil before serving.

Nutritional Value (Amount per Serving):

Calories: 38; Fat: 0.29; Carb: 8.62; Protein: 1.69

Slow Cooker Garlic Herb Roasted Vegetables

Prep Time: 15 Minutes   Cook Time: 4 Hours   Serves: 6

Ingredients:

- 1 lb baby potatoes, halved
- 2 cups baby carrots
- 2 cups Brussels sprouts, halved
- 1 red bell pepper, sliced
- 1 yellow bell pepper, sliced
- 3 cloves garlic, minced
- 2 tbsp olive oil
- 1 tsp dried thyme
- 1 tsp dried rosemary
- Salt and pepper to taste

Directions:

1. In a large bowl, combine all the vegetables and garlic.
2. Drizzle olive oil over the vegetables and toss to coat evenly.
3. Sprinkle thyme, rosemary, salt, and pepper, ensuring even distribution.
4. Transfer the seasoned vegetables to the slow cooker.
5. Cook on low for 4 hours, stirring once halfway through.
6. Serve warm as a delightful side dish.

Nutritional Value (Amount per Serving):

Calories: 123; Fat: 4.72; Carb: 18.79; Protein: 3.1

Crock Pot Quinoa Pilaf

Prep Time: 10 Minutes   Cook Time: 2 Hours 30 Minutes   Serves: 6

Ingredients:

- 1 cup quinoa, rinsed
- 2 cups vegetable broth
- 1 cup cherry tomatoes, halved
- 1 cup cucumber, diced
- 1/2 cup red onion, finely chopped
- 1/4 cup fresh parsley, chopped
- 2 tbsp olive oil
- 1 lemon, juiced
- Salt and pepper to taste

Directions:

1. Combine quinoa and vegetable broth in the slow cooker.
2. Add tomatoes, cucumber, and red onion.
3. Drizzle olive oil over the mixture and stir well.
4. Cook on low for 2.5 hours or until quinoa is tender.
5. Fluff the quinoa with a fork and stir in parsley.
6. Squeeze lemon juice over the pilaf and season with salt and pepper.
7. Serve as a flavorful and nutritious side dish.

Nutritional Value (Amount per Serving):

Calories: 162; Fat: 6.33; Carb: 22.4; Protein: 4.52

Sweet and Spicy Crock Pot Glazed Carrots

Prep Time: 10 Minutes   Cook Time: 3 Hours   Serves: 8

Ingredients:

- 2 lbs baby carrots
- 1/4 cup maple syrup
- 2 tbsp gluten-free soy sauce
- 1 tbsp Dijon mustard
- 2 cloves garlic, minced
- 1/2 tsp crushed red pepper flakes
- Salt and pepper to taste
- 2 tbsp fresh parsley, chopped (for garnish)

Directions:

1. Place baby carrots in the slow cooker.
2. In a bowl, whisk together maple syrup, soy sauce, Dijon mustard, garlic, and red pepper flakes.
3. Pour the sauce over the carrots, ensuring they are well-coated.
4. Cook on low for 3 hours or until carrots are tender.
5. Season with salt and pepper, garnish with parsley, and serve.

Calories: 73; Fat: 0.62; Carb: 17.37; Protein: 1.37

Creamy Crock Pot Mashed Cauliflower

Prep Time: 15 Minutes   Cook Time: 3 Hours   Serves: 4

Ingredients:

- 1 large head cauliflower, chopped
- 3 cloves garlic, peeled
- 1/4 cup chicken or vegetable broth
- 2 tbsp olive oil
- 1/4 cup unsweetened almond milk
- Salt and pepper to taste
- Chopped chives (for garnish)

Directions:

1. Place cauliflower and garlic in the slow cooker.
2. Drizzle olive oil and pour broth over the cauliflower.
3. Cook on low for 3 hours or until cauliflower is very tender.
4. Use a hand blender to puree the cauliflower until smooth.
5. Stir in almond milk and season with salt and pepper.
6. Garnish with chopped chives and serve as a creamy mashed cauliflower side dish.

Nutritional Value (Amount per Serving):

Calories: 101; Fat: 7.59; Carb: 7.46; Protein: 2.1

Crock Pot Balsamic Glazed Brussels Sprouts

Prep Time: 10 Minutes   Cook Time: 2 Hours 30 Minutes   Serves: 6

Ingredients:

- 1.5 lbs Brussels sprouts, trimmed and halved
- 1/4 cup balsamic vinegar
- 2 tbsp olive oil
- 2 tbsp honey
- 2 cloves garlic, minced
- Salt and pepper to taste
- 1/4 cup grated Parmesan cheese (optional)

Directions:

1. Place Brussels sprouts in the slow cooker.
2. In a bowl, whisk together balsamic vinegar, olive oil, honey, and garlic.
3. Pour the mixture over Brussels sprouts, ensuring even coating.
4. Cook on low for 2.5 hours or until sprouts are tender.

5. Season with salt and pepper, and sprinkle with Parmesan if desired.
6. Serve these flavorful Brussels sprouts as a gourmet side.

Nutritional Value (Amount per Serving):

Calories: 141; Fat: 6.02; Carb: 19.35; Protein: 5.3

Crock Pot Lemon Herb Asparagus

Prep Time: 10 Minutes   Cook Time: 2 Hours   Serves: 6

Ingredients:

- 1 lb asparagus, trimmed
- 2 tbsp olive oil
- 2 tbsp fresh lemon juice
- 2 cloves garlic, minced
- 1 tsp dried thyme
- Salt and pepper to taste
- Lemon zest for garnish

Directions:

1. Place asparagus in the slow cooker.
2. In a bowl, whisk together olive oil, lemon juice, garlic, thyme, salt, and pepper.
3. Pour the mixture over asparagus, ensuring even coating.
4. Cook on low for 2 hours or until asparagus is tender.
5. Garnish with lemon zest before serving.

Nutritional Value (Amount per Serving):

Calories: 62; Fat: 4.64; Carb: 4.91; Protein: 1.93

Slow Cooker Mexican Street Corn

Prep Time: 15 Minutes   Cook Time: 3 Hours   Serves: 8

Ingredients:

- 6 cups frozen corn kernels
- 1/2 cup mayonnaise
- 1/2 cup sour cream
- 1 cup cotija cheese, crumbled
- 1/4 cup fresh cilantro, chopped
- 1 tsp chili powder
- 1 lime, cut into wedges

Directions:

1. In the slow cooker, combine corn, mayonnaise, sour cream, and cotija cheese.
2. Stir well to coat the corn evenly.
3. Cook on low for 3 hours.
4. Sprinkle with cilantro and chili powder before serving.
5. Serve with lime wedges for an extra burst of flavor.

Nutritional Value (Amount per Serving):

Calories: 254; Fat: 11.48; Carb: 29.94; Protein: 8.06

Crock Pot Butternut Squash Soup

Prep Time: 20 Minutes   Cook Time: 4 Hours   Serves: 6

Ingredients:

- 1 medium butternut squash, peeled and cubed
- 1 apple, peeled and diced
- 1 onion, chopped
- 3 cups vegetable broth
- 1 tsp ground cinnamon
- 1/2 tsp ground nutmeg
- Salt and pepper to taste
- 1/2 cup coconut milk (optional, for creaminess)

Directions:

1. Place butternut squash, apple, onion, vegetable broth, cinnamon, and nutmeg in the slow cooker.
2. Season with salt and pepper.
3. Cook on low for 4 hours or until vegetables are tender.
4. Use a blender to puree the soup until smooth.
5. Stir in coconut milk if desired.
6. Adjust seasoning and serve hot.

Nutritional Value (Amount per Serving):

Calories: 91; Fat: 4.95; Carb: 12.39; Protein: 1.15

Crock Pot Cauliflower and Broccoli Gratin

Prep Time: 15 Minutes   Cook Time: 3 Hours   Serves: 6

Ingredients:

- 1 head cauliflower, cut into florets
- 1 bunch broccoli, cut into florets
- 1 cup shredded cheddar cheese
- 1 cup shredded mozzarella cheese
- 1 cup gluten-free breadcrumbs
- 2 cups milk (dairy or plant-based)
- 3 tbsp gluten-free all-purpose flour
- 3 tbsp butter

- 1 tsp Dijon mustard
- Salt and pepper to taste
- Chopped fresh parsley for garnish

Directions:

1. In a saucepan, melt butter over medium heat. Whisk in gluten-free flour until a paste forms.
2. Slowly add milk, whisking continuously to avoid lumps.
3. Stir in Dijon mustard and continue to cook until the sauce thickens.
4. In the slow cooker, layer cauliflower and broccoli florets.
5. Pour the sauce over the vegetables.
6. In a bowl, mix together cheddar and mozzarella cheeses with gluten-free breadcrumbs. Sprinkle over the vegetables.
7. Cook on low for 3 hours or until vegetables are tender and the top is golden.
8. Garnish with chopped parsley before serving.

Nutritional Value (Amount per Serving):

Calories: 214; Fat: 9.82; Carb: 18.26; Protein: 14.44

Crock Pot Spinach and Artichoke Dip

Prep Time: 10 Minutes   Cook Time: 2 Hours   Serves: 8

Ingredients:

- 2 cups frozen chopped spinach, thawed and drained
- 1 can (14 oz) artichoke hearts, drained and chopped
- 1 cup mayonnaise
- 1 cup sour cream
- 1 cup shredded Parmesan cheese
- 1 cup shredded mozzarella cheese
- 2 cloves garlic, minced
- Salt and pepper to taste
- Gluten-free tortilla chips or vegetable sticks for dipping

Directions:

1. In the slow cooker, combine spinach, artichoke hearts, mayonnaise, sour cream, Parmesan, mozzarella, and garlic.
2. Stir well and season with salt and pepper.
3. Cook on low for 2 hours or until the cheese is melted and the dip is heated through.
4. Stir before serving with gluten-free tortilla chips or vegetable sticks.

Nutritional Value (Amount per Serving):

Calories: 355; Fat: 21.94; Carb: 26.25; Protein: 14.49

Crock Pot Spicy Sweet Potato Wedges

Prep Time: 15 Minutes   Cook Time: 3 Hours   Serves: 6

Ingredients:

- 3 sweet potatoes, cut into wedges
- 2 tbsp olive oil
- 1 tsp paprika
- 1/2 tsp cayenne pepper
- 1 tsp ground cumin
- 1 tsp garlic powder
- Salt and pepper to taste
- Fresh cilantro for garnish

Directions:

1. In a bowl, toss sweet potato wedges with olive oil, paprika, cayenne pepper, cumin, garlic powder, salt, and pepper.
2. Transfer the seasoned wedges to the slow cooker.
3. Cook on low for 3 hours or until sweet potatoes are tender.
4. Garnish with fresh cilantro before serving.

Nutritional Value (Amount per Serving):

Calories: 82; Fat: 5.1; Carb: 8.89; Protein: 2.45

Crock Pot Mediterranean Stuffed Peppers

Prep Time: 20 Minutes   Cook Time: 4 Hours   Serves: 8

Ingredients:

- 4 large bell peppers, halved and seeds removed
- 1 cup cooked quinoa
- 1 can (15 oz) chickpeas, drained and rinsed
- 1 cup diced cucumber
- 1 cup cherry tomatoes, halved
- 1/2 cup Kalamata olives, chopped
- 1/2 cup crumbled feta cheese
- 2 tbsp olive oil
- 2 tbsp red wine vinegar
- 1 tsp dried oregano
- Salt and pepper to taste
- Fresh parsley for garnish

Directions:

1. In a bowl, combine cooked quinoa, chickpeas, cucumber, tomatoes, olives, feta, olive oil, red wine vinegar, oregano, salt, and pepper.

2. Stuff each bell pepper half with the quinoa mixture.
3. Place stuffed peppers in the slow cooker.
4. Cook on low for 4 hours or until peppers are tender.
5. Garnish with fresh parsley before serving.

Nutritional Value (Amount per Serving):

Calories: 151; Fat: 7.59; Carb: 16.37; Protein: 5.34

Crock Pot Maple Glazed Acorn Squash

Prep Time: 15 Minutes   Cook Time: 3 Hours   Serves: 6

Ingredients:

- 2 acorn squashes, sliced
- 1/4 cup maple syrup
- 2 tbsp olive oil
- 1 tsp ground cinnamon
- 1/2 tsp ground nutmeg
- Salt and pepper to taste
- Chopped pecans for garnish

Directions:

1. Arrange acorn squash slices in the slow cooker.
2. In a bowl, whisk together maple syrup, olive oil, cinnamon, nutmeg, salt, and pepper.
3. Pour the mixture over the squash, ensuring even coating.
4. Cook on low for 3 hours or until squash is fork-tender.
5. Garnish with chopped pecans before serving.

Nutritional Value (Amount per Serving):

Calories: 262; Fat: 17.81; Carb: 27.44; Protein: 3

Crock Pot Garlic Herb Butter Mushrooms

Prep Time: 10 Minutes   Cook Time: 2 Hours   Serves: 6

Ingredients:

- 1 lb mushrooms, cleaned and halved
- 1/2 cup unsalted butter, melted
- 3 cloves garlic, minced
- 1 tsp dried thyme
- 1 tsp dried rosemary
- Salt and pepper to taste
- Fresh parsley for garnish

Directions:

1. In the slow cooker, combine mushrooms, melted butter, garlic, thyme, and

rosemary.

2. Toss well to coat the mushrooms.
3. Cook on low for 2 hours or until mushrooms are tender.
4. Season with salt and pepper.
5. Garnish with fresh parsley before serving.

Nutritional Value (Amount per Serving):

Calories: 323; Fat: 11.07; Carb: 58.28; Protein: 8.13

Crock Pot Buffalo Cauliflower Bites

Prep Time: 15 Minutes   Cook Time: 3 Hours   Serves: 6

Ingredients:

- 1 head cauliflower, cut into florets
- 1/2 cup gluten-free flour
- 1/2 cup water
- 1 tsp garlic powder
- 1 tsp onion powder
- 1/2 cup buffalo sauce
- 2 tbsp melted butter
- Ranch or blue cheese dressing for dipping

Directions:

1. In a bowl, whisk together gluten-free flour, water, garlic powder, and onion powder to create a batter.
2. Dip cauliflower florets into the batter, coating them evenly.
3. Arrange battered cauliflower in the slow cooker.
4. In a separate bowl, mix buffalo sauce and melted butter.
5. Pour the buffalo sauce mixture over the cauliflower.
6. Cook on low for 3 hours or until cauliflower is crispy.
7. Serve with ranch or blue cheese dressing for dipping.

Nutritional Value (Amount per Serving):

Calories: 110; Fat: 5.46; Carb: 14.79; Protein: 1.44

Chapter 6: Soups, Stews and Chilis

Slow Cooker Minestrone Soup

Prep Time: 20 Minutes   Cook Time: 6 Hours   Serves: 6-8

Ingredients:

- 2 cups gluten-free pasta, cooked separately
- 1 can (14 oz) diced tomatoes
- 2 carrots, peeled and sliced
- 2 celery stalks, chopped
- 1 zucchini, diced
- 1 onion, finely chopped
- 3 cloves garlic, minced
- 6 cups gluten-free vegetable broth
- 1 can (15 oz) cannellini beans, drained and rinsed
- 1 teaspoon dried oregano
- 1 teaspoon dried basil
- Salt and pepper to taste
- Fresh basil for garnish

Directions:

1. Combine cooked pasta, diced tomatoes, carrots, celery, zucchini, onion, and garlic in the slow cooker.
2. Add vegetable broth, cannellini beans, oregano, basil, salt, and pepper. Stir well.
3. Cook on low for 6 hours.
4. Adjust seasoning if needed and serve hot, garnished with fresh basil.

Nutritional Value (Amount per Serving):

Calories: 129; Fat: 1.34; Carb: 26; Protein: 4.44

Slow Cooker Chicken and Quinoa Soup

Prep Time: 15 Minutes   Cook Time: 4 Hours   Serves: 6-8

Ingredients:

- 1 lb boneless, skinless chicken breasts, diced
- 1 cup quinoa, rinsed
- 4 carrots, peeled and chopped
- 4 celery stalks, chopped
- 1 onion, finely chopped
- 4 cloves garlic, minced
- 8 cups gluten-free chicken broth
- 1 teaspoon dried thyme

- Salt and pepper to taste
- Fresh parsley for garnish

1. In a skillet, sauté onions and garlic until translucent.
2. Add diced chicken to the skillet and brown on all sides.
3. Transfer the chicken, onions, and garlic to the slow cooker.
4. Add quinoa, carrots, celery, thyme, salt, and pepper.
5. Pour in the chicken broth and stir well.
6. Cook on low for 4 hours.
7. Adjust seasoning if needed and serve hot, garnished with fresh parsley.

Nutritional Value (Amount per Serving):

Calories: 248; Fat: 5.93; Carb: 36.93; Protein: 12.19

Vegetarian Lentil and Spinach Stew

Prep Time: 20 Minutes   Cook Time: 6 Hours   Serves: 6-8

Ingredients:

- 2 cups dry green lentils, rinsed
- 1 onion, diced
- 3 carrots, sliced
- 3 celery stalks, chopped
- 4 cloves garlic, minced
- 1 can (14 oz) diced tomatoes
- 6 cups gluten-free vegetable broth
- 2 teaspoons ground cumin
- 1 teaspoon smoked paprika
- Salt and pepper to taste
- 4 cups fresh spinach

Directions:

1. Combine lentils, onion, carrots, celery, garlic, tomatoes, broth, cumin, paprika, salt, and pepper in the slow cooker.
2. Stir well and cook on low for 6 hours.
3. Add fresh spinach during the last 30 minutes of cooking.
4. Adjust seasoning if needed and serve warm.

Nutritional Value (Amount per Serving):

Calories: 58; Fat: 3.3; Carb: 12.44; Protein: 0.48

Beef and Sweet Potato Chili

Prep Time: 25 Minutes   Cook Time: 8 Hours   Serves: 6-8

Ingredients:

- 2 lbs lean ground beef
- 2 sweet potatoes, peeled and diced

- 1 onion, finely chopped
- 3 cloves garlic, minced
- 2 cans (14 oz each) diced tomatoes
- 1 can (15 oz) black beans, drained and rinsed
- 1 can (15 oz) kidney beans, drained and rinsed
- 1 cup gluten-free beef broth
- 2 tablespoons chili powder
- 1 tablespoon cumin
- Salt and pepper to taste
- Chopped green onions for garnish

Directions:

1. In a skillet, brown ground beef with onion and garlic; drain excess fat.
2. Transfer beef mixture to the slow cooker.
3. Add sweet potatoes, diced tomatoes, black beans, kidney beans, beef broth, chili powder, cumin, salt, and pepper. Mix well.
4. Cook on low for 8 hours.
5. Adjust seasoning if needed and serve hot, garnished with chopped green onions.

Nutritional Value (Amount per Serving):

Calories: 447; Fat: 17.47; Carb: 29.42; Protein: 43.09

Turkey and Vegetable Soup

Prep Time: 15 Minutes   Cook Time: 5 Hours   Serves: 6-8

Ingredients:

- 1 lb ground turkey
- 4 carrots, peeled and sliced
- 3 parsnips, peeled and chopped
- 1 cup green beans, chopped
- 1 onion, diced
- 3 cloves garlic, minced
- 8 cups gluten-free turkey or chicken broth
- 1 teaspoon dried thyme
- 1 bay leaf
- Salt and pepper to taste
- Fresh parsley for garnish

Directions:

1. Brown ground turkey in a skillet; drain excess fat.
2. Transfer turkey to the slow cooker and add carrots, parsnips, green beans, onion, and garlic.

3. Pour in turkey or chicken broth, add thyme, bay leaf, salt, and pepper.
4. Cook on low for 5 hours.
5. Remove bay leaf, adjust seasoning if needed, and serve hot, garnished with fresh parsley.

Nutritional Value (Amount per Serving):

Calories: 140; Fat: 5.78; Carb: 7.44; Protein: 15.49

Spicy Butternut Squash Soup

Prep Time: 20 Minutes   Cook Time: 6 Hours   Serves: 6-8

Ingredients:

- 1 medium butternut squash, peeled, seeded, and diced
- 2 carrots, peeled and chopped
- 1 apple, peeled, cored, and chopped
- 1 onion, diced
- 4 cups gluten-free vegetable broth
- 1 teaspoon ground cinnamon
- 1/2 teaspoon ground nutmeg
- 1/2 teaspoon cayenne pepper
- Salt and pepper to taste
- Coconut milk for garnish

Directions:

1. Combine butternut squash, carrots, apple, onion, broth, cinnamon, nutmeg, cayenne pepper, salt, and pepper in the slow cooker.
2. Cook on low for 6 hours.
3. Use an immersion blender to puree the soup until smooth.
4. Adjust seasoning if needed and serve hot, drizzled with coconut milk.

Nutritional Value (Amount per Serving):

Calories: 77; Fat: 1.23; Carb: 17.3; Protein: 1.31

Chicken and Wild Rice Stew

Prep Time: 15 Minutes   Cook Time: 7 Hours   Serves: 6-8

Ingredients:

- 1 lb boneless, skinless chicken thighs
- 1 cup wild rice, rinsed
- 4 carrots, peeled and sliced
- 3 celery stalks, chopped

- 1 onion, diced
- 3 cloves garlic, minced
- 8 cups gluten-free chicken broth
- 1 teaspoon dried thyme
- 1/2 teaspoon dried rosemary
- Salt and pepper to taste
- Fresh parsley for garnish

Directions:

1. Place chicken thighs, wild rice, carrots, celery, onion, and garlic in the slow cooker.
2. Pour in chicken broth and add thyme, rosemary, salt, and pepper. Mix well.
3. Cook on low for 7 hours.
4. Shred chicken with a fork, adjust seasoning if needed, and serve hot, garnished with fresh parsley

Nutritional Value (Amount per Serving):

Calories: 224; Fat: 4.59; Carb: 34.86; Protein: 11.67

Black Bean and Quinoa Chili

Prep Time: 20 Minutes   Cook Time: 5 Hours   Serves: 6-8

Ingredients:

- 2 cups quinoa, rinsed
- 2 cans (15 oz each) black beans, drained and rinsed
- 1 can (14 oz) diced tomatoes
- 1 onion, finely chopped
- 3 cloves garlic, minced
- 1 red bell pepper, diced
- 4 cups gluten-free vegetable broth
- 2 tablespoons chili powder
- 1 teaspoon ground cumin
- Salt and pepper to taste
- Avocado slices for garnish

Directions:

1. Combine quinoa, black beans, diced tomatoes, onion, garlic, bell pepper, vegetable broth, chili powder, cumin, salt, and pepper in the slow cooker.
2. Stir well and cook on low for 5 hours.
3. Adjust seasoning if needed and serve hot, topped with avocado slices.

Nutritional Value (Amount per Serving):

Calories: 417; Fat: 8.32; Carb: 69.46; Protein: 19.28

Turkey and Quinoa Meatball Soup

Prep Time: 30 Minutes   Cook Time: 4 Hours   Serves: 6-8

Ingredients:

- 1 lb ground turkey
- 1/2 cup quinoa, cooked separately
- 2 carrots, peeled and sliced
- 2 celery stalks, chopped
- 1 onion, diced
- 3 cloves garlic, minced
- 8 cups gluten-free turkey or chicken broth
- 1 teaspoon dried thyme
- 1/2 teaspoon dried sage
- Salt and pepper to taste
- Fresh dill for garnish

Directions:

1. In a bowl, mix ground turkey with cooked quinoa, forming small meatballs.
2. Place turkey and quinoa meatballs, carrots, celery, onion, and garlic in the slow cooker.
3. Pour in turkey or chicken broth and add thyme, sage, salt, and pepper. Mix well.
4. Cook on low for 4 hours.
5. Adjust seasoning if needed and serve hot, garnished with fresh dill.

Nutritional Value (Amount per Serving):

Calories: 143; Fat: 5.91; Carb: 7.11; Protein: 15.7

Sweet Potato and Coconut Curry Soup

Prep Time: 25 Minutes   Cook Time: 6 Hours   Serves: 6-8

Ingredients:

- 2 large sweet potatoes, peeled and diced
- 1 onion, finely chopped
- 3 cloves garlic, minced
- 1 can (14 oz) coconut milk
- 4 cups gluten-free vegetable broth
- 2 teaspoons curry powder
- 1 teaspoon ground turmeric
- Salt and pepper to taste
- Fresh cilantro for garnish

Directions:

1. Combine sweet potatoes, onion, garlic, coconut milk, vegetable broth, curry powder, turmeric, salt, and pepper in the slow cooker.
2. Stir well and cook on low for 6 hours.
3. Use an immersion blender to puree the soup until smooth.

4. Adjust seasoning if needed and serve hot, garnished with fresh cilantro.

Nutritional Value (Amount per Serving):

Calories: 197; Fat: 13.72; Carb: 18.62; Protein: 2.84

Lentil and Vegetable Stew

Prep Time: 15 Minutes   Cook Time: 6 Hours   Serves: 6-8

Ingredients:

- 2 cups dried green or brown lentils, rinsed
- 3 carrots, peeled and sliced
- 2 celery stalks, chopped
- 1 onion, diced
- 3 cloves garlic, minced
- 1 can (14 oz) diced tomatoes
- 8 cups gluten-free vegetable broth
- 1 teaspoon ground coriander
- 1 teaspoon smoked paprika
- Salt and pepper to taste
- Fresh parsley for garnish

Directions:

1. Combine lentils, carrots, celery, onion, garlic, diced tomatoes, vegetable broth, coriander, smoked paprika, salt, and pepper in the slow cooker.
2. Stir well and cook on low for 6 hours.
3. Adjust seasoning if needed and serve hot, garnished with fresh parsley.

Nutritional Value (Amount per Serving):

Calories: 54; Fat: 0.28; Carb: 12.23; Protein: 2.68

Italian Sausage and Kale Soup

Prep Time: 20 Minutes   Cook Time: 4 Hours   Serves: 6-8

Ingredients:

- 1 lb gluten-free Italian sausage, casings removed
- 1 onion, finely chopped
- 3 carrots, peeled and sliced
- 3 potatoes, peeled and diced
- 4 cups gluten-free chicken broth
- 1 can (14 oz) crushed tomatoes
- 4 cups chopped kale

- 2 teaspoons Italian seasoning
- Salt and pepper to taste
- Grated Parmesan for garnish

Directions:

1. In a skillet, brown the Italian sausage, breaking it into crumbles; drain excess fat.
2. Transfer sausage to the slow cooker and add onion, carrots, potatoes, chicken broth, crushed tomatoes, kale, Italian seasoning, salt, and pepper. Mix well.
3. Cook on low for 4 hours.
4. Adjust seasoning if needed and serve hot, garnished with grated Parmesan.

Nutritional Value (Amount per Serving):

Calories: 320; Fat: 12.43; Carb: 39.33; Protein: 17.35

Moroccan Chickpea Stew

Prep Time: 20 Minutes   Cook Time: 6 Hours   Serves: 6-8

Ingredients:

- 2 cans (15 oz each) chickpeas, drained and rinsed
- 1 butternut squash, peeled, seeded, and diced
- 1 onion, finely chopped
- 3 cloves garlic, minced
- 4 cups gluten-free vegetable broth
- 1 can (14 oz) diced tomatoes
- 1 teaspoon ground cumin
- 1 teaspoon ground coriander
- 1/2 teaspoon cinnamon
- Salt and pepper to taste
- Chopped fresh cilantro for garnish

Directions:

1. Combine chickpeas, butternut squash, onion, garlic, vegetable broth, diced tomatoes, cumin, coriander, cinnamon, salt, and pepper in the slow cooker.
2. Stir well and cook on low for 6 hours.
3. Adjust seasoning if needed and serve hot, garnished with chopped fresh cilantro.

Nutritional Value (Amount per Serving):

Calories: 235; Fat: 4.59; Carb: 38.74; Protein: 12.94

Thai Coconut Chicken Soup

Prep Time: 20 Minutes   Cook Time: 4 Hours   Serves: 4-6

Ingredients:

- 1 lb boneless, skinless chicken breasts, thinly sliced
- 1 red bell pepper, thinly sliced
- 1 onion, finely chopped
- 3 cloves garlic, minced
- 1 can (14 oz) coconut milk
- 4 cups gluten-free chicken broth
- 2 tablespoons gluten-free soy sauce
- 1 tablespoon red curry paste
- 1 tablespoon fresh ginger, grated
- Salt and pepper to taste
- Fresh cilantro and lime wedges for garnish

Directions:

1. Combine sliced chicken, bell pepper, onion, garlic, coconut milk, chicken broth, soy sauce, red curry paste, ginger, salt, and pepper in the slow cooker.
2. Stir well and cook on low for 4 hours.
3. Adjust seasoning if needed and serve hot, garnished with fresh cilantro and lime wedges.

Nutritional Value (Amount per Serving):

Calories: 396; Fat: 26.38; Carb: 29.7; Protein: 13.78

Black-Eyed Pea and Ham Soup

Prep Time: 25 Minutes   Cook Time: 6 Hours   Serves: 6-8

Ingredients:

- 2 cups dried black-eyed peas, soaked overnight and drained
- 1 lb ham, diced
- 3 carrots, peeled and sliced
- 2 celery stalks, chopped
- 1 onion, diced
- 3 cloves garlic, minced
- 8 cups gluten-free chicken broth
- 1 teaspoon dried thyme
- 1 bay leaf
- Salt and pepper to taste

- Chopped fresh parsley for garnish

Directions:

1. Combine black-eyed peas, diced ham, carrots, celery, onion, garlic, chicken broth, thyme, bay leaf, salt, and pepper in the slow cooker.
2. Stir well and cook on low for 6 hours.
3. Remove bay leaf, adjust seasoning if needed, and serve hot, garnished with chopped fresh parsley.

Nutritional Value (Amount per Serving):

Calories: 132; Fat: 3.37; Carb: 10.79; Protein: 15.49

Tomato Basil Quinoa Soup

Prep Time: 20 Minutes   Cook Time: 4 Hours   Serves: 4-6

Ingredients:

- 1 cup quinoa, rinsed
- 1 can (28 oz) crushed tomatoes
- 1 onion, finely chopped
- 3 carrots, peeled and sliced
- 4 cups gluten-free vegetable broth
- 1/2 cup fresh basil, chopped
- 1 teaspoon dried oregano
- Salt and pepper to taste
- Grated Parmesan for garnish

Directions:

1. Combine quinoa, crushed tomatoes, onion, carrots, vegetable broth, fresh basil, oregano, salt, and pepper in the slow cooker.
2. Stir well and cook on low for 4 hours.
3. Adjust seasoning if needed and serve hot, garnished with grated Parmesan.

Nutritional Value (Amount per Serving):

Calories: 159; Fat: 2.28; Carb: 29.22; Protein: 6.03

Chapter 7: Casseroles and Gluten-Free Pasta

Gluten-Free Mexican Chicken Enchilada Casserole

Prep Time: 25 Minutes   Cook Time: 4 Hours   Serves: 6

Ingredients:

- 2 cups shredded cooked chicken
- 2 cups gluten-free corn and rice blend pasta, cooked
- 1 can (15 oz) black beans, drained and rinsed
- 1 cup corn kernels (fresh or frozen)
- 1 cup gluten-free enchilada sauce
- 1 cup shredded Mexican cheese blend
- 1 teaspoon ground cumin
- 1 teaspoon chili powder
- Salt and pepper to taste
- Fresh cilantro, chopped (for garnish)

Directions:

1. In the crock pot, layer cooked chicken, cooked pasta, black beans, and corn.
2. Sprinkle ground cumin, chili powder, salt, and pepper over the layers.
3. Pour gluten-free enchilada sauce evenly over the layers.
4. Sprinkle shredded Mexican cheese blend on top.
5. Cover and cook on low for 4 hours.
6. Before serving, garnish with chopped fresh cilantro.
7. Allow the enchilada casserole to rest for a few minutes before serving.

Nutritional Value (Amount per Serving):

Calories: 425; Fat: 22.35; Carb: 36.19; Protein: 20.71

Gluten-Free Chicken and Vegetable Casserole

Prep Time: 20 Minutes   Cook Time: 4 Hours   Serves: 6-8

Ingredients:

- 2 pounds boneless, skinless chicken breasts, cut into bite-sized pieces
- 2 cups gluten-free pasta (your choice), uncooked
- 2 cups broccoli florets
- 1 cup carrots, sliced
- 1 cup bell peppers (mix of red and green), diced
- 1 cup gluten-free chicken broth
- 1 cup gluten-free cream of mushroom soup
- 1 cup shredded cheddar cheese
- 1/2 cup grated Parmesan cheese
- 1 tablespoon olive oil

- 1 teaspoon garlic powder
- 1 teaspoon dried thyme
- Salt and pepper to taste
- Fresh parsley, chopped (for garnish)

Directions:

1. Cut chicken into bite-sized pieces. Slice carrots, dice bell peppers, and chop broccoli into florets. Grate Parmesan cheese and shred cheddar cheese.
2. Heat olive oil in a large skillet over medium-high heat. Season chicken pieces with garlic powder, dried thyme, salt, and pepper.
3. Sauté chicken until browned on all sides, about 5 minutes.
4. In the crock pot, layer uncooked gluten-free pasta at the bottom. Add browned chicken on top of the pasta. Place broccoli, carrots, and bell peppers evenly over the chicken.
5. In a bowl, mix gluten-free chicken broth and gluten-free cream of mushroom soup until well combined. Pour the soup mixture over the layered ingredients in the crock pot.
6. Set the crock pot on low heat and cook for 4 hours or until chicken is cooked through and vegetables are tender.
7. Sprinkle shredded cheddar and grated Parmesan cheese over the casserole during the last 30 minutes of cooking.
8. Once the cheese is melted and bubbly, turn off the crock pot. Garnish with fresh chopped parsley before serving.
9. Serve this gluten-free chicken and vegetable casserole hot and enjoy a delicious, hassle-free meal!

Nutritional Value (Amount per Serving):

Calories: 389; Fat: 14.53; Carb: 45.66; Protein: 19.28

Gluten-Free Beef and Mushroom Casserole

Prep Time: 20 Minutes   Cook Time: 4 Hours   Serves: 8

Ingredients:

- 2 pounds gluten-free ground beef
- 2 cups gluten-free spiral pasta, cooked
- 1 cup mushrooms, sliced
- 1 onion, diced
- 2 cups gluten-free beef broth
- 1 cup gluten-free tomato sauce
- 1 teaspoon dried oregano
- 1 teaspoon dried basil
- Salt and pepper to taste

- 1 cup shredded mozzarella cheese

Directions:

1. In a large bowl, mix cooked pasta, browned beef, mushrooms, onion, beef broth, tomato sauce, oregano, basil, salt, and pepper.
2. Transfer the mixture to the crock pot.
3. Cook on low for 4 hours.
4. Sprinkle shredded mozzarella on top during the last 30 minutes of cooking.
5. Allow the casserole to rest for a few minutes before serving.

Nutritional Value (Amount per Serving):

Calories: 363; Fat: 16.21; Carb: 19.04; Protein: 34.14

Gluten-Free Beef and Vegetable Pasta Casserole

Prep Time: 20 Minutes   Cook Time: 6 Hours   Serves: 8

Ingredients:

- 2 pounds gluten-free ground beef
- 2 cups gluten-free rotini pasta, uncooked
- 1 onion, diced
- 2 bell peppers (any color), diced
- 2 cups gluten-free marinara sauce
- 1 cup gluten-free beef broth
- 1 teaspoon dried Italian seasoning
- Salt and pepper to taste
- 1 cup shredded cheddar cheese

Directions:

1. In a skillet, brown the ground beef over medium heat. Drain excess fat.
2. In the crock pot, mix together cooked ground beef, uncooked rotini pasta, diced onion, diced bell peppers, marinara sauce, beef broth, Italian seasoning, salt, and pepper.
3. Cook on low for 6 hours or until pasta is tender.
4. Sprinkle shredded cheddar cheese over the casserole during the last 30 minutes of cooking.
5. Allow the casserole to rest for a few minutes before serving.

Nutritional Value (Amount per Serving):

Calories: 373; Fat: 17.48; Carb: 21.34; Protein: 32.23

Gluten-Free Mediterranean Quinoa Casserole

Prep Time: 15 Minutes   Cook Time: 3 Hours   Serves: 4

Ingredients:

- 1 cup quinoa, rinsed
- 2 cups gluten-free vegetable broth

- 1 can (14 oz) diced tomatoes, drained
- 1 cup artichoke hearts, chopped
- 1 cup Kalamata olives, sliced
- 1 cup gluten-free chickpeas, drained and rinsed
- 1 teaspoon dried oregano
- 1 teaspoon dried basil
- Salt and pepper to taste
- 1 cup crumbled feta cheese

Directions:

1. In the crock pot, combine quinoa, vegetable broth, diced tomatoes, artichoke hearts, olives, chickpeas, oregano, basil, salt, and pepper.
2. Cook on low for 3 hours or until quinoa is cooked and flavors are well combined.
3. Sprinkle crumbled feta cheese over the casserole during the last 15 minutes of cooking.
4. Allow the casserole to cool for a few minutes before serving.

Nutritional Value (Amount per Serving):

Calories: 385; Fat: 15.31; Carb: 48.32; Protein: 16.27

Crock Pot Gluten-Free Lasagna Casserole

Prep Time: 20 Minutes   Cook Time: 4 Hours   Serves: 6-8

Ingredients:

- 2 cups gluten-free lasagna noodles, broken into pieces
- 1 pound gluten-free ground beef
- 1 onion, finely chopped
- 2 cloves garlic, minced
- 1 can (28 oz) crushed tomatoes
- 1 can (14 oz) diced tomatoes, drained
- 1 cup gluten-free tomato sauce
- 1 teaspoon dried oregano
- 1 teaspoon dried basil
- Salt and pepper to taste
- 2 cups ricotta cheese
- 1 egg, beaten
- 2 cups shredded mozzarella cheese
- 1/2 cup grated Parmesan cheese
- Fresh basil, chopped (for garnish)

Directions:

1. Break gluten-free lasagna noodles into smaller pieces, following package

instructions.

2. In a skillet, brown the ground beef over medium heat. Add chopped onions and minced garlic, cooking until onions are translucent. Drain excess fat.
3. In a bowl, mix together crushed tomatoes, diced tomatoes, tomato sauce, oregano, basil, salt, and pepper.
4. In the crock pot, layer broken lasagna noodles, cooked ground beef mixture, and tomato sauce mixture.
5. In a separate bowl, combine ricotta cheese and beaten egg.
6. Spoon dollops of the ricotta mixture over the layers in the crock pot.
7. Sprinkle shredded mozzarella and grated Parmesan cheese on top.
8. Cover and cook on low for 4 hours or until noodles are tender.
9. Before serving, sprinkle fresh chopped basil on top.
10. Allow the lasagna casserole to rest for a few minutes before serving.

Nutritional Value (Amount per Serving):

Calories: 460; Fat: 21.95; Carb: 24.53; Protein: 40.61

Gluten-Free Caprese Quinoa Casserole

Prep Time: 25 Minutes   Cook Time: 4 Hours   Serves: 4

Ingredients:

- 1 cup quinoa, rinsed
- 2 cups gluten-free vegetable broth
- 1 cup gluten-free marinara sauce
- 1 cup cherry tomatoes, halved
- 1 cup fresh mozzarella balls, halved
- 1/2 cup gluten-free basil pesto
- 1/4 cup grated Parmesan cheese
- Salt and pepper to taste
- Fresh basil, chopped (for garnish)

Directions:

1. In the crock pot, combine rinsed quinoa and vegetable broth.
2. Stir in gluten-free marinara sauce.
3. Add halved cherry tomatoes and fresh mozzarella balls on top.
4. Spoon dollops of gluten-free basil pesto throughout the casserole.
5. Sprinkle grated Parmesan cheese over the top. Season with salt and pepper.
6. Cover and cook on low for 4 hours.
7. Before serving, garnish with chopped fresh basil.
8. Allow the Caprese quinoa casserole to rest for a few minutes before serving.

Nutritional Value (Amount per Serving):

Calories: 228; Fat: 4.59; Carb: 38.93; Protein: 9.5

Gluten-Free Pesto Chicken and Vegetable Casserole

Prep Time: 20 Minutes   Cook Time: 4 Hours   Serves: 6

Ingredients:

- 2 cups gluten-free fusilli pasta, cooked
- 2 cups cooked chicken, shredded
- 1 cup cherry tomatoes, halved
- 1 cup zucchini, diced
- 1 cup gluten-free chicken broth
- 1/2 cup gluten-free basil pesto
- 1/2 cup grated Parmesan cheese
- 1/4 cup gluten-free all-purpose flour
- 1/4 cup unsalted butter
- 1 cup gluten-free milk
- Salt and pepper to taste
- Fresh basil, chopped (for garnish)

Directions:

1. In the crock pot, layer cooked fusilli pasta, shredded chicken, cherry tomatoes, and diced zucchini.
2. In a saucepan, melt butter. Whisk in gluten-free flour until smooth.
3. Gradually add gluten-free milk, stirring until the mixture thickens.
4. Stir in gluten-free basil pesto and grated Parmesan cheese. Season with salt and pepper.
5. Pour the pesto cream sauce evenly over the layers in the crock pot.
6. Cover and cook on low for 4 hours.
7. Before serving, garnish with chopped fresh basil.
8. Allow the pesto chicken and vegetable casserole to rest for a few minutes before serving.

Nutritional Value (Amount per Serving):

Calories: 344; Fat: 23.2; Carb: 20.84; Protein: 13.14

Gluten-Free Ratatouille and Quinoa Casserole

Prep Time: 25 Minutes   Cook Time: 4 Hours   Serves: 6

Ingredients:

- 1 cup quinoa, rinsed
- 2 cups gluten-free vegetable broth
- 1 eggplant, diced
- 1 zucchini, diced
- 1 bell pepper, diced
- 1 cup cherry tomatoes, halved
- 1 cup gluten-free marinara sauce
- 1 teaspoon dried thyme
- 1 teaspoon dried rosemary
- Salt and pepper to taste
- 1/4 cup gluten-free olive oil
- 1/2 cup crumbled feta cheese
- Fresh basil, chopped (for garnish)

Directions:

1. In the crock pot, combine rinsed quinoa and vegetable broth.

2. Layer diced eggplant, diced zucchini, diced bell pepper, and halved cherry tomatoes over the quinoa.
3. Pour gluten-free marinara sauce over the vegetables. Sprinkle dried thyme and dried rosemary. Season with salt and pepper.
4. Drizzle gluten-free olive oil over the top.
5. Cover and cook on low for 4 hours.
6. Sprinkle crumbled feta cheese on top during the last 30 minutes of cooking.
7. Before serving, garnish with chopped fresh basil.
8. Allow the ratatouille and quinoa casserole to rest for a few minutes before serving.

Nutritional Value (Amount per Serving):

Calories: 219; Fat: 8.54; Carb: 29.74; Protein: 7.76

Spinach and Artichoke Pasta Casserole

Prep Time: 20 Minutes   Cook Time: 3 Hours   Serves: 6

Ingredients:

- 2 cups gluten-free fusilli pasta, cooked
- 1 cup fresh spinach, chopped
- 1 can (14 oz) artichoke hearts, drained and chopped
- 1 cup gluten-free Alfredo sauce
- 1 cup gluten-free vegetable broth
- 1 cup shredded mozzarella cheese
- 1/2 cup grated Parmesan cheese
- 1 teaspoon garlic powder
- Salt and pepper to taste

Directions:

1. In the crock pot, layer cooked fusilli pasta, chopped spinach, and chopped artichoke hearts.
2. In a bowl, mix together gluten-free Alfredo sauce, gluten-free vegetable broth, garlic powder, salt, and pepper.
3. Pour the sauce over the layers in the crock pot.
4. Sprinkle shredded mozzarella and grated Parmesan cheese on top.
5. Cover and cook on low for 3 hours.
6. Allow the spinach and artichoke pasta casserole to rest for a few minutes before serving.

Nutritional Value (Amount per Serving):

Calories: 321; Fat: 21.53; Carb: 19.9; Protein: 13.75

Teriyaki Chicken and Vegetable Noodle Casserole

Prep Time: 25 Minutes   Cook Time: 4 Hours   Serves: 6

Ingredients:

- 2 cups gluten-free rice noodles, cooked
- 2 cups cooked chicken, shredded
- 1 cup broccoli florets
- 1 cup snap peas, trimmed
- 1 carrot, julienned
- 1/2 cup gluten-free teriyaki sauce
- 1/4 cup gluten-free soy sauce
- 2 tablespoons honey
- 1 tablespoon sesame oil
- 1 teaspoon ginger, minced
- 1 teaspoon garlic, minced
- 2 green onions, sliced (for garnish)
- Sesame seeds (for garnish)

Directions:

1. In the crock pot, layer cooked rice noodles, shredded chicken, broccoli florets, snap peas, and julienned carrot.
2. In a bowl, whisk together gluten-free teriyaki sauce, gluten-free soy sauce, honey, sesame oil, minced ginger, and minced garlic.
3. Pour the teriyaki sauce over the layers in the crock pot.
4. Cover and cook on low for 4 hours.
5. Before serving, garnish with sliced green onions and sesame seeds.
6. Allow the teriyaki chicken and vegetable noodle casserole to cool slightly before serving.

Nutritional Value (Amount per Serving):

Calories: 329; Fat: 18.71; Carb: 28.44; Protein: 12.14

Pesto Veggie and Chicken Quinoa Casserole

Prep Time: 20 Minutes   Cook Time: 3 Hours   Serves: 4

Ingredients:

- 1 cup quinoa, rinsed
- 2 cups gluten-free chicken broth
- 2 cups cooked chicken, diced
- 1 cup cherry tomatoes, halved
- 1 cup zucchini, diced
- 1/2 cup gluten-free basil pesto
- 1/4 cup grated Parmesan cheese
- Salt and pepper to taste
- Fresh basil, chopped (for garnish)

Directions:

1. In the crock pot, combine rinsed quinoa and gluten-free chicken broth.
2. Add diced cooked chicken, halved cherry tomatoes, and diced zucchini to the crock pot.
3. Stir in gluten-free basil pesto. Mix well.
4. Season with salt and pepper.

5. Cover and cook on low for 3 hours.
6. Sprinkle grated Parmesan cheese over the casserole during the last 30 minutes of cooking.
7. Before serving, garnish with chopped fresh basil.
8. Allow the pesto veggie and chicken quinoa casserole to rest for a few minutes before serving.

Nutritional Value (Amount per Serving):

Calories: 452; Fat: 27.42; Carb: 30.26; Protein: 20.41

Gluten-Free Sausage and Mushroom Penne Bake

Prep Time: 25 Minutes   Cook Time: 4 Hours   Serves: 6

Ingredients:

- 2 cups gluten-free penne pasta, cooked
- 1 pound gluten-free Italian sausage, casings removed
- 1 onion, diced
- 2 cloves garlic, minced
- 1 cup mushrooms, sliced
- 1 can (14 oz) gluten-free crushed tomatoes
- 1 cup gluten-free marinara sauce
- 1 teaspoon dried oregano
- 1 teaspoon dried basil
- Salt and pepper to taste
- 1 cup shredded mozzarella cheese
- 1/2 cup grated Parmesan cheese
- Fresh parsley, chopped (for garnish)

Directions:

1. In a skillet, brown the gluten-free Italian sausage over medium heat. Break it into crumbles. Drain excess fat.
2. Add diced onion, minced garlic, and sliced mushrooms to the skillet. Sauté until vegetables are softened.
3. In the crock pot, combine cooked penne pasta, browned sausage, sautéed vegetables, crushed tomatoes, marinara sauce, dried oregano, dried basil, salt, and pepper.
4. Sprinkle shredded mozzarella and grated Parmesan cheese on top.
5. Cover and cook on low for 4 hours.
6. Before serving, garnish with chopped fresh parsley.
7. Allow the sausage and mushroom penne bake to rest for a few minutes before serving.

Nutritional Value (Amount per Serving):

Calories: 349; Fat: 16.69; Carb: 29.84; Protein: 25.37

Gluten-Free Ratatouille Chicken and Rice Casserole

Prep Time: 30 Minutes   Cook Time: 4 Hours   Serves: 6

Ingredients:

- 2 cups cooked chicken, shredded
- 1 cup gluten-free rice, cooked
- 1 eggplant, diced
- 1 zucchini, diced
- 1 bell pepper, diced
- 1 cup cherry tomatoes, halved
- 1 can (14 oz) gluten-free diced tomatoes
- 1 teaspoon dried thyme
- 1 teaspoon dried rosemary
- Salt and pepper to taste
- 1/4 cup gluten-free olive oil
- 1/2 cup crumbled feta cheese
- Fresh basil, chopped (for garnish)

Directions:

1. In the crock pot, layer shredded cooked chicken, cooked rice, diced eggplant, diced zucchini, diced bell pepper, cherry tomatoes, and diced tomatoes.
2. Sprinkle dried thyme and dried rosemary over the layers. Season with salt and pepper.
3. Drizzle gluten-free olive oil over the top.
4. Cover and cook on low for 4 hours.
5. Sprinkle crumbled feta cheese on top during the last 30 minutes of cooking.
6. Before serving, garnish with chopped fresh basil.
7. Allow the ratatouille chicken and rice casserole to rest for a few minutes before serving.

Nutritional Value (Amount per Serving):

Calories: 301; Fat: 22.12; Carb: 14.53; Protein: 12.13

Chapter 8: Appetizers and Snacks

Quinoa and Black Bean Stuffed Peppers

Prep Time: 20 Minutes   Cook Time: 3 Hours   Serves: 6-8

Ingredients:

- 6 large bell peppers, halved and seeds removed
- 1 cup cooked quinoa
- 1 can (15 ounces) black beans, drained and rinsed
- 1 cup corn kernels (fresh or frozen)
- 1 cup diced tomatoes
- 1 cup shredded cheddar cheese
- 1 teaspoon ground cumin
- 1 teaspoon chili powder
- Salt and pepper to taste
- Fresh cilantro for garnish

Directions:

1. In a bowl, combine cooked quinoa, black beans, corn, diced tomatoes, shredded cheddar, cumin, chili powder, salt, and pepper.
2. Stuff each pepper half with the quinoa mixture.
3. Arrange stuffed peppers in the slow cooker.
4. Cook on low for 3 hours or until peppers are tender.
5. Garnish with fresh cilantro before serving.

Nutritional Value (Amount per Serving):

Calories: 178; Fat: 2.68; Carb: 30.51; Protein: 10.2

Spinach and Artichoke Dip

Prep Time: 15 Minutes   Cook Time: 2 Hours   Serves: 6-8

Ingredients:

- 1 (10-ounce) package frozen chopped spinach, thawed and drained
- 1 (14-ounce) can artichoke hearts, drained and chopped
- 1 cup mayonnaise
- 1 cup grated Parmesan cheese
- 1 cup shredded mozzarella cheese
- 2 cloves garlic, minced
- 1 teaspoon onion powder
- Salt and pepper to taste
- Tortilla chips or gluten-free crackers for serving

Directions:

1. In a large bowl, combine the drained spinach, chopped artichoke hearts,

mayonnaise, Parmesan cheese, mozzarella cheese, minced garlic, and onion powder.
2. Season the mixture with salt and pepper to taste. Stir well to ensure even distribution of ingredients.
3. Transfer the mixture to the slow cooker and cook on low for 2 hours or until hot and bubbly.
4. Stir the dip occasionally during cooking to prevent sticking to the sides.
5. Once done, serve the spinach and artichoke dip warm with gluten-free tortilla chips or crackers.

Nutritional Value (Amount per Serving):

Calories: 228; Fat: 15.86; Carb: 9.69; Protein: 12.22

Buffalo Chicken Wings

Prep Time: 10 Minutes   Cook Time: 3 Hours   Serves: 6-8

Ingredients:

- 3 pounds chicken wings, split at joints, tips discarded
- 1 cup gluten-free hot sauce
- 1/2 cup unsalted butter
- 1 teaspoon garlic powder
- 1 teaspoon onion powder
- 1 teaspoon dried oregano
- 1 teaspoon paprika
- Celery sticks and ranch dressing for serving

Directions:

1. Place the chicken wings in the slow cooker.
2. In a saucepan over medium heat, melt the butter and stir in the hot sauce, garlic powder, onion powder, oregano, and paprika.
3. Pour the sauce over the chicken wings, ensuring they are evenly coated.
4. Cover and cook on low for 3 hours or until the wings are cooked through and tender.
5. Serve the Buffalo chicken wings with celery sticks and ranch dressing.

Nutritional Value (Amount per Serving):

Calories: 358; Fat: 17.73; Carb: 3.61; Protein: 44.03

Mediterranean Stuffed Mushrooms

Prep Time: 20 Minutes   Cook Time: 2 Hours 30 Minutes   Serves: 4-6

Ingredients:

- 24 large button mushrooms, cleaned and stems removed
- 1/2 cup gluten-free breadcrumbs
- 1/2 cup crumbled feta cheese
- 1/4 cup chopped sun-dried tomatoes
- 2 tablespoons chopped fresh parsley
- 2 cloves garlic, minced
- 2 tablespoons olive oil
- Salt and pepper to taste

Directions:

1. In a bowl, mix together the gluten-free breadcrumbs, feta cheese, sun-dried tomatoes, parsley, minced garlic, and olive oil.
2. Season the mixture with salt and pepper to taste.
3. Stuff each mushroom cap with the mixture and place them in the slow cooker.
4. Cook on low for 2.5 hours or until the mushrooms are tender.
5. Serve the Mediterranean stuffed mushrooms warm.

Nutritional Value (Amount per Serving):

Calories: 136; Fat: 9.15; Carb: 9.53; Protein: 6.46

Sweet and Spicy Meatballs

Prep Time: 15 Minutes   Cook Time: 4 Hours   Serves: 8-10

Ingredients:

- 2 pounds ground beef or turkey
- 1 cup gluten-free breadcrumbs
- 2 eggs, beaten
- 1 cup gluten-free barbecue sauce
- 1/2 cup apricot preserves
- 2 tablespoons gluten-free soy sauce
- 1 teaspoon crushed red pepper flakes
- Green onions, chopped, for garnish (optional)

Directions:

1. In a large bowl, combine the ground meat, breadcrumbs, and beaten eggs. Form the mixture into meatballs.
2. In a separate bowl, mix together the barbecue sauce, apricot preserves, soy sauce, and crushed red pepper flakes.
3. Place the meatballs in the slow cooker and pour the sauce over them, ensuring even coating.

4. Cook on low for 4 hours or until the meatballs are cooked through.

5. Garnish with chopped green onions if desired before serving.

Nutritional Value (Amount per Serving):

Calories: 325; Fat: 16.33; Carb: 13.58; Protein: 29.47

Caprese Skewers with Balsamic Glaze

Prep Time: 15 Minutes   Cook Time: 1 Hour   Serves: 4-6

Ingredients:

- 1 pint cherry tomatoes
- 1 pound fresh mozzarella balls
- Fresh basil leaves
- 1/4 cup balsamic glaze
- Wooden skewers

Directions:

1. Thread a tomato, a mozzarella ball, and a basil leaf onto each skewer, repeating until all ingredients are used.
2. Arrange the skewers in the slow cooker.
3. Drizzle the balsamic glaze over the skewers.
4. Cover and cook on low for 1 hour or until the mozzarella is slightly melted.
5. Serve the Caprese skewers warm.

Nutritional Value (Amount per Serving):

Calories: 32; Fat: 0.24; Carb: 7.7; Protein: 0.84

Cranberry and Rosemary Meatballs

Prep Time: 15 Minutes   Cook Time: 2 Hours 30 Minutes   Serves: 8-10

Ingredients:

- 2 pounds ground chicken or turkey
- 1 cup gluten-free breadcrumbs
- 1/2 cup dried cranberries, chopped
- 2 tablespoons fresh rosemary, minced
- 2 cloves garlic, minced
- 1 teaspoon salt
- 1/2 teaspoon black pepper
- 1 cup cranberry sauce (store-bought or homemade)
- 1/4 cup gluten-free soy sauce

Directions:

1. In a large bowl, combine ground meat, breadcrumbs, cranberries, rosemary, garlic, salt, and pepper. Form into meatballs.

2. Place the meatballs in the slow cooker.
3. In a separate bowl, mix cranberry sauce and soy sauce. Pour over the meatballs.
4. Cook on low for 2.5 hours or until meatballs are cooked through.
5. Serve with toothpicks for easy snacking.

Nutritional Value (Amount per Serving):

Calories: 373; Fat: 26.58; Carb: 23.12; Protein: 10.99

Zucchini Parmesan Crisps

Prep Time: 15 Minutes   Cook Time: 2 Hours   Serves: 4-6

Ingredients:

- 2 large zucchinis, thinly sliced
- 1 cup gluten-free breadcrumbs
- 1/2 cup grated Parmesan cheese
- 1 teaspoon dried oregano
- 1 teaspoon garlic powder
- 1/2 teaspoon salt
- 1/4 teaspoon black pepper
- 2 large eggs, beaten
- Marinara sauce for dipping

Directions:

1. In a bowl, combine breadcrumbs, Parmesan, oregano, garlic powder, salt, and pepper.
2. Dip zucchini slices into beaten eggs, then coat with the breadcrumb mixture.
3. Arrange coated zucchini slices in the slow cooker.
4. Cook on low for 2 hours or until the zucchini is crispy.
5. Serve with marinara sauce for dipping.

Nutritional Value (Amount per Serving):

Calories: 652; Fat: 53.75; Carb: 7.74; Protein: 34.57

Bacon-Wrapped Jalapeño Poppers

Prep Time: 25 Minutes   Cook Time: 2 Hours 30 Minutes   Serves: 6-8

Ingredients:

- 12 large jalapeño peppers, halved and seeds removed
- 8 ounces cream cheese, softened
- 1 cup shredded cheddar cheese
- 12 slices gluten-free bacon, cut in half
- Toothpicks

Directions:

1. In a bowl, mix cream cheese and shredded cheddar until well combined.

2. Stuff each jalapeño half with the cheese mixture.
3. Wrap each stuffed jalapeño with a half-slice of bacon and secure with a toothpick.
4. Arrange the poppers in the slow cooker.
5. Cook on low for 2.5 hours or until the bacon is crispy.
6. Serve these delightful poppers warm.

Nutritional Value (Amount per Serving):

Calories: 318; Fat: 27.46; Carb: 9.44; Protein: 10.23

Sesame Ginger Edamame

Prep Time: 10 Minutes   Cook Time: 1 Hour 30 Minutes   Serves: 4-6

Ingredients:

- 2 cups frozen edamame, thawed
- 2 tablespoons gluten-free soy sauce
- 1 tablespoon sesame oil
- 1 tablespoon rice vinegar
- 1 tablespoon honey
- 1 teaspoon fresh ginger, grated
- 1 tablespoon sesame seeds
- Green onions, sliced, for garnish

Directions:

1. In a bowl, whisk together soy sauce, sesame oil, rice vinegar, honey, and grated ginger.
2. Toss the thawed edamame with the sauce mixture.
3. Transfer the edamame to the slow cooker.
4. Cook on low for 1.5 hours, stirring occasionally.
5. Sprinkle sesame seeds and sliced green onions on top before serving.

Nutritional Value (Amount per Serving):

Calories: 133; Fat: 7.06; Carb: 11.61; Protein: 7.84

Gluten-Free Stuffed Mushrooms

Prep Time: 20 Minutes   Cook Time: 2 Hours 30 Minutes   Serves: 6-8

Ingredients:

- 24 large mushrooms, cleaned and stems removed
- 1/2 pound gluten-free Italian sausage, cooked and crumbled
- 1 cup cream cheese, softened
- 1/4 cup grated Parmesan cheese
- 2 cloves garlic, minced
- 2 tablespoons fresh parsley, chopped

- Salt and pepper to taste

1. In a bowl, combine cooked sausage, cream cheese, Parmesan, minced garlic, chopped parsley, salt, and pepper.
2. Stuff each mushroom cap with the sausage and cheese mixture.
3. Arrange the stuffed mushrooms in the slow cooker.
4. Cook on low for 2.5 hours or until mushrooms are tender.
5. Serve warm.

Nutritional Value (Amount per Serving):

Calories: 249; Fat: 19.94; Carb: 6.61; Protein: 12.3

Caprese Quinoa Salad

Prep Time: 15 Minutes   Cook Time: 2 Hours   Serves: 4-6

Ingredients:

- 1 cup cooked quinoa
- 1 pint cherry tomatoes, halved
- 1 cup fresh mozzarella balls
- 1/4 cup fresh basil leaves, chopped
- 2 tablespoons balsamic glaze
- Salt and pepper to taste

Directions:

1. In a large bowl, combine cooked quinoa, cherry tomatoes, mozzarella balls, chopped basil, balsamic glaze, salt, and pepper.
2. Transfer the quinoa salad to the slow cooker.
3. Cook on low for 2 hours, stirring occasionally.
4. Serve the Caprese quinoa salad at room temperature.

Nutritional Value (Amount per Serving):

Calories: 69; Fat: 0.9; Carb: 13.58; Protein: 2.61

Sun-Dried Tomato and Olive Tapenade

Prep Time: 15 Minutes   Cook Time: 1 Hour   Serves: 4-6

Ingredients:

- 1 cup Kalamata olives, pitted and chopped
- 1/2 cup sun-dried tomatoes, chopped
- 2 cloves garlic, minced
- 2 tablespoons capers, drained
- 1/4 cup fresh parsley, chopped
- 2 tablespoons olive oil
- Juice of 1 lemon

- Gluten-free crackers for serving

Directions:

1. In a bowl, combine chopped olives, sun-dried tomatoes, minced garlic, capers, chopped parsley, olive oil, and lemon juice.
2. Transfer the tapenade to the slow cooker.
3. Cook on low for 1 hour, stirring occasionally.
4. Allow the tapenade to cool before serving with gluten-free crackers.

Nutritional Value (Amount per Serving):

Calories: 102; Fat: 8.68; Carb: 6.5; Protein: 1.31

Gluten-Free Pigs in a Blanket

Prep Time: 15 Minutes   Cook Time: 2 Hours   Serves: 8-10

Ingredients:

- 1 package gluten-free cocktail sausages
- 1 cup gluten-free biscuit mix
- 1/3 cup milk (or dairy-free alternative)
- 1/4 cup melted butter (or dairy-free alternative)
- 1 tablespoon Dijon mustard
- 1 teaspoon dried thyme
- Gluten-free ketchup and mustard for dipping

Directions:

1. In a bowl, mix biscuit mix, milk, melted butter, Dijon mustard, and dried thyme to form a dough.
2. Roll out the dough on a lightly floured surface and cut into strips.
3. Wrap each cocktail sausage with a strip of dough, securing the ends.
4. Place the wrapped sausages in the slow cooker.
5. Cook on low for 2 hours or until the dough is golden brown.
6. Serve with gluten-free ketchup and mustard for dipping.

Nutritional Value (Amount per Serving):

Calories: 156; Fat: 12.21; Carb: 6.44; Protein: 7.31

Chapter 9: Desserts

Banana Bread Pudding

Prep Time: 15 Minutes   Cook Time: 3 Hours   Serves: 8

Ingredients:

- 4 ripe bananas, mashed
- 6 cups gluten-free bread cubes
- 2 cups almond milk
- 4 large eggs
- 1/2 cup maple syrup
- 1 teaspoon vanilla extract
- 1/2 teaspoon cinnamon
- 1/4 teaspoon nutmeg
- 1/4 cup chopped walnuts
- Powdered sugar for dusting

Directions:

1. In a bowl, combine mashed bananas, almond milk, eggs, maple syrup, vanilla extract, cinnamon, and nutmeg.
2. Place gluten-free bread cubes in the slow cooker and pour the banana mixture over them. Let it sit for 10 minutes.
3. Sprinkle chopped walnuts on top.
4. Cover and cook on low for 3 hours. Dust with powdered sugar before serving.

Nutritional Value (Amount per Serving):

Calories: 265; Fat: 8.47; Carb: 43.91; Protein: 4.97

Slow Cooker Chocolate Lava Cake

Prep Time: 15 Minutes   Cook Time: 2 Hours   Serves: 6

Ingredients:

- 1 cup gluten-free all-purpose flour
- 1/2 cup unsweetened cocoa powder
- 1 cup granulated sugar
- 1/2 teaspoon baking powder
- 1/4 teaspoon salt
- 1/2 cup unsalted butter, melted
- 1/2 cup milk
- 1 teaspoon vanilla extract
- 1/2 cup chocolate chips
- 1/2 cup hot water

Directions:

1. In a bowl, whisk together gluten-free flour, cocoa powder, sugar, baking powder, and salt.
2. Stir in melted butter, milk, and vanilla extract until well combined.
3. Fold in chocolate chips and pour the batter into a greased slow cooker.

4. In a separate bowl, mix hot water and an additional tablespoon of cocoa powder. Pour over the batter in the slow cooker.
5. Cover and cook on low for 2 hours or until the edges are set and the center is slightly gooey.
6. Serve warm.

Nutritional Value (Amount per Serving):

Calories: 323; Fat: 14.82; Carb: 46; Protein: 5.32

Cinnamon Apple Crisp

Prep Time: 20 Minutes   Cook Time: 3 Hours   Serves: 8

Ingredients:

- 6 cups sliced and peeled apples
- 1/2 cup granulated sugar
- 1 teaspoon ground cinnamon
- 1/4 teaspoon nutmeg
- 1 cup gluten-free oats
- 1/2 cup almond flour
- 1/2 cup melted coconut oil
- 1/4 cup honey
- 1/2 teaspoon vanilla extract

Directions:

1. In a large bowl, toss apples with sugar, cinnamon, and nutmeg. Place the mixture in the slow cooker.
2. In another bowl, combine oats, almond flour, melted coconut oil, honey, and vanilla extract.
3. Spread the oat mixture over the apples in the slow cooker.
4. Cover and cook on low for 3 hours or until the apples are tender.
5. Serve with a scoop of vanilla ice cream if desired.

Nutritional Value (Amount per Serving):

Calories: 248; Fat: 14.66; Carb: 34.39; Protein: 2.31

Pumpkin Spice Rice Pudding

Prep Time: 10 Minutes   Cook Time: 4 Hours   Serves: 6

Ingredients:

- 2 cups cooked white rice
- 1 can (15 oz) pumpkin puree
- 2 cups coconut milk
- 1/2 cup maple syrup
- 1 teaspoon pumpkin spice
- 1/4 teaspoon salt

- 1/2 cup raisins
- 1/4 cup chopped pecans (optional)

Directions:

1. In the slow cooker, combine cooked rice, pumpkin puree, coconut milk, maple syrup, pumpkin spice, and salt.
2. Stir in raisins and set the slow cooker to low.
3. Cook for 4 hours, stirring occasionally.
4. Serve warm, sprinkled with chopped pecans if desired.

Nutritional Value (Amount per Serving):

Calories: 667; Fat: 36; Carb: 75.77; Protein: 16.8

Berry Cobbler with Almond Flour Topping

Prep Time: 15 Minutes   Cook Time: 2 Hours 30 Minutes   Serves: 8

Ingredients:

- 4 cups mixed berries (strawberries, blueberries, raspberries)
- 1/2 cup granulated sugar
- 1 tablespoon cornstarch
- 1 cup almond flour
- 1/2 cup gluten-free oats
- 1/4 cup melted butter
- 1/4 cup honey
- 1/2 teaspoon vanilla extract
- 1/4 teaspoon salt

Directions:

1. In a bowl, toss berries with sugar and cornstarch. Place in the slow cooker.
2. In another bowl, combine almond flour, oats, melted butter, honey, vanilla extract, and salt.
3. Crumble the almond flour mixture over the berries in the slow cooker.
4. Cover and cook on low for 2.5 hours or until the berries are bubbling and the topping is golden brown.

Nutritional Value (Amount per Serving):

Calories: 291; Fat: 14.06; Carb: 42.36; Protein: 2.6

Coconut Rice Pudding with Mango

Prep Time: 10 Minutes   Cook Time: 3 Hours   Serves: 6

Ingredients:

- 1 cup Arborio rice
- 1 can (13.5 oz) coconut milk
- 2 cups almond milk
- 1/2 cup sugar
- 1/2 teaspoon vanilla extract
- 1/2 cup shredded coconut
- 1 ripe mango, diced

Directions:

1. Rinse Arborio rice under cold water and place it in the slow cooker.
2. Add coconut milk, almond milk, sugar, and vanilla extract. Stir well.
3. Cover and cook on low for 3 hours, stirring occasionally.
4. Toast shredded coconut in a dry pan until golden brown.
5. Serve rice pudding topped with diced mango and toasted coconut.

Nutritional Value (Amount per Serving):

Calories: 303; Fat: 20.45; Carb: 34.03; Protein: 4.96

Cinnamon Apple Crisp

Prep Time: 20 Minutes   Cook Time: 3 Hours   Serves: 8

Ingredients:

- 6 cups sliced and peeled apples
- 1/2 cup granulated sugar
- 1 teaspoon ground cinnamon
- 1/4 teaspoon nutmeg
- 1 cup gluten-free oats
- 1/2 cup almond flour
- 1/2 cup melted coconut oil
- 1/4 cup honey
- 1/2 teaspoon vanilla extract

Directions:

1. In a bowl, combine mashed bananas, almond milk, eggs, maple syrup, vanilla extract, cinnamon, and nutmeg.
2. Place gluten-free bread cubes in the slow cooker and pour the banana mixture over them. Let it sit for 10 minutes.
3. Sprinkle chopped walnuts on top.
4. Cover and cook on low for 3 hours. Dust with powdered sugar before serving.

Nutritional Value (Amount per Serving):

Calories: 248; Fat: 14.66; Carb: 34.39; Protein: 2.31

Lemon Blueberry Cheesecake

Prep Time: 20 Minutes   Cook Time: 3 Hours   Serves: 8

Ingredients:

- 2 cups gluten-free graham cracker crumbs
- 1/2 cup melted butter
- 16 oz cream cheese, softened
- 1 cup sugar
- 4 large eggs

- 1/2 cup sour cream
- 1/4 cup fresh lemon juice
- 1 teaspoon lemon zest
- 1 cup fresh blueberries

Directions:

1. Mix graham cracker crumbs with melted butter and press into the bottom of the slow cooker to form the crust.
2. In a bowl, beat cream cheese and sugar until smooth. Add eggs one at a time, beating well after each addition.
3. Stir in sour cream, lemon juice, and lemon zest. Fold in blueberries.
4. Pour the mixture over the crust in the slow cooker.
5. Cover and cook on low for 3 hours. Chill before serving.

Nutritional Value (Amount per Serving):

Calories: 411; Fat: 32.03; Carb: 26.33; Protein: 6.49

Chocolate Peanut Butter Fondue

Prep Time: 10 Minutes   Cook Time: 1 Hour   Serves: 6

Ingredients:

- 1 cup chocolate chips
- 1/2 cup creamy peanut butter
- 1/2 cup coconut milk
- 1 teaspoon vanilla extract
- Assorted gluten-free dippables (strawberries, marshmallows, banana slices)

Directions:

1. In the slow cooker, combine chocolate chips, peanut butter, coconut milk, and vanilla extract.
2. Cover and cook on low for 1 hour, stirring occasionally until smooth.
3. Serve the chocolate peanut butter fondue with your favorite gluten-free dippables.

Nutritional Value (Amount per Serving):

Calories: 306; Fat: 20.24; Carb: 28.43; Protein: 6.8

Cherry Almond Crumble Bars

Prep Time: 20 Minutes   Cook Time: 2 Hours 30 Minutes   Serves: 12

Ingredients:

- 2 cups gluten-free rolled oats
- 1 cup almond flour

- 1/2 cup melted coconut oil
- 1/2 cup maple syrup
- 1/2 teaspoon almond extract
- 1 can (21 oz) cherry pie filling
- 1/2 cup sliced almonds

Directions:

1. In a bowl, combine oats, almond flour, melted coconut oil, maple syrup, and almond extract to form the crust.
2. Press half of the mixture into the bottom of the slow cooker.
3. Spread cherry pie filling over the crust.
4. Sprinkle the remaining oat mixture on top and add sliced almonds.
5. Cover and cook on low for 2.5 hours. Allow to cool before cutting into bars.

Nutritional Value (Amount per Serving):

Calories: 209; Fat: 10.33; Carb: 33.03; Protein: 2.94

Peach and Pecan Cobbler

Prep Time: 15 Minutes   Cook Time: 3 Hours   Serves: 8

Ingredients:

- 4 cups sliced fresh peaches
- 1 cup chopped pecans
- 1/2 cup granulated sugar
- 1 teaspoon ground cinnamon
- 1 cup gluten-free all-purpose flour
- 1/2 cup almond flour
- 1/2 cup melted butter
- 1/2 cup almond milk
- 1 teaspoon vanilla extract

Directions:

1. In a bowl, combine sliced peaches, chopped pecans, sugar, and cinnamon. Place the mixture in the slow cooker.
2. In another bowl, mix gluten-free all-purpose flour, almond flour, melted butter, almond milk, and vanilla extract until well combined.
3. Drop spoonfuls of the batter over the peach mixture.
4. Cover and cook on low for 3 hours or until the peaches are tender and the topping is golden brown.

Nutritional Value (Amount per Serving):

Calories: 376; Fat: 20.93; Carb: 47.76; Protein: 3.58

Carrot Cake Oatmeal

Prep Time: 15 Minutes   Cook Time: 4 Hours   Serves: 6

Ingredients:

- 2 cups grated carrots
- 1 cup gluten-free rolled oats

- 1/2 cup raisins
- 1/2 cup chopped walnuts
- 1 teaspoon ground cinnamon
- 1/4 teaspoon ground nutmeg
- 4 cups almond milk
- 1/4 cup maple syrup
- 1 teaspoon vanilla extract

Directions:

1. In the slow cooker, combine grated carrots, rolled oats, raisins, chopped walnuts, cinnamon, and nutmeg.
2. Stir in almond milk, maple syrup, and vanilla extract.
3. Cover and cook on low for 4 hours. Stir well before serving.

Nutritional Value (Amount per Serving):

Calories: 215; Fat: 7.59; Carb: 39.14; Protein: 5.11

Mint Chocolate Pudding Cake

Prep Time: 20 Minutes　　Cook Time: 2 Hours　　Serves: 8

Ingredients:

- 1 cup gluten-free all-purpose flour
- 1/2 cup unsweetened cocoa powder
- 1 1/2 teaspoons baking powder
- 1/4 teaspoon salt
- 1/2 cup sugar
- 1/2 cup milk
- 1/4 cup melted butter
- 1 teaspoon peppermint extract
- 1/2 cup chocolate chips
- 1 cup hot water
- Fresh mint leaves for garnish (optional)

Directions:

1. In a bowl, whisk together gluten-free flour, cocoa powder, baking powder, salt, and sugar.
2. Stir in milk, melted butter, and peppermint extract until well combined.
3. Fold in chocolate chips and spread the batter evenly in the slow cooker.
4. In a separate bowl, mix hot water and an additional tablespoon of cocoa powder. Pour over the batter in the slow cooker.
5. Cover and cook on low for 2 hours or until the cake is set. Garnish with fresh mint leaves if desired.

Nutritional Value (Amount per Serving):

Calories: 187; Fat: 8.61; Carb: 26.98; Protein: 3.75

Coconut Mango Rice Pudding

Prep Time: 15 Minutes   Cook Time: 3 Hours   Serves: 6

Ingredients:

- 1 cup Arborio rice
- 1 can (13.5 oz) coconut milk
- 2 cups almond milk
- 1/2 cup sugar
- 1/2 teaspoon vanilla extract
- 1 cup diced fresh mango
- 1/4 cup shredded coconut

Directions:

1. Rinse Arborio rice under cold water and place it in the slow cooker.
2. Add coconut milk, almond milk, sugar, and vanilla extract. Stir well.
3. Gently fold in diced mango.
4. Cover and cook on low for 3 hours, stirring occasionally.
5. Serve rice pudding topped with shredded coconut.

Nutritional Value (Amount per Serving):

Calories: 301; Fat: 20.43; Carb: 33.66; Protein: 4.89

Chocolate Covered Strawberry Fondue

Prep Time: 15 Minutes   Cook Time: 1 Hour 30 Minutes   Serves: 6

Ingredients:

- 1 cup dark chocolate chips
- 1/2 cup coconut milk
- 1 teaspoon vanilla extract
- 1 pound fresh strawberries, hulled
- Gluten-free marshmallows for dipping

Directions:

1. In the slow cooker, combine dark chocolate chips, coconut milk, and vanilla extract.
2. Cover and cook on low for 1.5 hours, stirring occasionally until smooth.
3. Serve the chocolate fondue with fresh strawberries and gluten-free marshmallows for dipping.

Nutritional Value (Amount per Serving):

Calories: 162; Fat: 9.82; Carb: 17.95; Protein: 1.76

Cranberry Orange Quinoa Cookies

Prep Time: 15 Minutes   Cook Time: 2 Hours   Serves: 12

Ingredients:

- 1 cup cooked quinoa, cooled

- 1 cup almond flour
- 1/2 cup dried cranberries, chopped
- 1/4 cup coconut oil, melted
- 1/4 cup maple syrup
- Zest of one orange
- 1 teaspoon vanilla extract
- 1/2 teaspoon baking soda
- 1/4 teaspoon salt
- 1/4 cup chopped pecans

Directions:

1. In a large bowl, combine cooked quinoa, almond flour, chopped cranberries, melted coconut oil, maple syrup, orange zest, vanilla extract, baking soda, and salt. Mix until well combined.
2. Fold in chopped pecans.
3. Line the slow cooker with parchment paper. Scoop tablespoon-sized portions of the cookie dough onto the parchment paper.
4. Cover and cook on low for 2 hours or until the cookies are set.
5. Allow the cookies to cool before serving.

Nutritional Value (Amount per Serving):

Calories: 98; Fat: 6.39; Carb: 9.94; Protein: 0.92

APPENDIX RECIPE INDEX

Made in United States
Troutdale, OR
11/22/2024

25172443R10064